Trade4Profits

Watch Me Trade 2

Book 3 of the Trade4Profits Series

Jim D. Dawson

www.trade4profits.com

Facebook: www.facebook.com/Trade4Profits-1700359833625590

Twitter: trade4profits1

ISBN: 9781795056076

TITLE: Trade4Profits – Watch Me Trade 2

AUTHOR: Jim D. Dawson

PUBLISHER: J.D. Dawson

www.trade4profits.com

Facebook: www.facebook.com/Trade4Profits-1700359833625590/.com

Twitter: trade4profits1

Disclaimer

There are lot's of books out there about how to trade, some even written by me. But, there are not a lot of books that let you see the trades as you will see them when you are trading. Trading is about greed and fear. Fear of losing money and greed of making money. When you start to lose money you either say "I must get out now before I lose more" or even more dangerously "I must stay in until it turns around." When you are making money you must fight the desire to take a profit while you have it or the desire to make even more if you just wait.

Typically if you wait for it to turn around you lose more money. If you do not take profits, they have a habit of going away. That is why it is important to trade a trading plan. Know why you are getting into a trade, when you need to get out (or defend) and when you need to take profits (either full or partial). This is your trading plan. Always trade your plan, do not change it during the trade.

So, how do you know when to change your trading plan? First of all, as I said before, not during the trade. You refine your trading by keeping a trading journal. You review your old trades frequently. Identify what you did wrong and what you did right.

Some of the gross money received on my trades may seem low even though the return is good. Please keep in mind that most of these trades can be scaled up utilizing additional contracts/shares to bring in more gross money. One of the reasons I sometimes use less contracts is because of other positions I have open using the equity and/or margin in my account. I do not trade just one trade at a time, I usually have multiple positions open with varying expiration dates.

I debated about whether or not to show commissions in my trades. The problem is that although there will always be commissions they can vary greatly between accounts. I have trading accounts with four different brokers and all the commissions are different. I took a middle of the road approach and decided to show commissions on some trades but not on others. You can tell the ones that do not have commissions included by the total prices.

When describing the trades I am only using their stock symbol. It would be good for you to know what these stocks are in order to fully understand how they trade. Stocks, ETF's and Indexes behave differently and typically have different volatility and option prices.

I discuss this more in Trade4Profits – Shortcuts to Profitable Trading, if you have not read that book I highly recommend it. Yes, I could give you their names and describe them for you but trading takes work and this is part of that. You will remember them more if you look them up for yourself.

I would also recommend that if you have a charting program that will show you the period I am trading that you pull the charts up. That way you will be able to get a better idea what I was seeing while I was trading. Try not to look at what happened after my trade until you see why I entered when I did. Then scroll forward and see what I traded through.

I know some of my trades in the book appear differently in the way I account for buying and selling. The truth is, sometimes I go back and forth in the way I keep up with my positions. Seems like sometimes one way makes sense, the I decide another way of tracking the trades make more sense. I thought about standardizing my trades for the book but then decided not to. The whole idea of the book is for you to see what I was seeing and thinking during the trades. That includes not being able to make up my mind the best way to document them. Don't worry, it will not be difficult for you to follow. If it was unclear I put the profit or loss in a way easy to understand at the end.

These are not all of my trades during this time period, I skipped around some to make sure you got a good example of my trades and thinking. You will see gains and losses in the book. Overall, the percentage of gains and losses you see here are about the same if I included every trade I made.

If you are not an experienced trader (and even if you are) I urge you to paper trade before ever trading with real money. I also encourage you to use a good trade calculator to see where positions are profitable, where they are break even, what your total risk is and what is your maximum profit and where. Although I use a number of different brokers, TDAmeritrade has my favorite trade calculator.

POSITION SIZES: **One thing you will notice is I show 1 or 2 contracts a lot of the time. I do this for a couple of reasons. One is that I don't want you to focus on "I could have made xxxxx" I want you to focus on how these trades work. Another is to help keep my personal portfolio values confidential. I base my position sizes in my portfolio balance as compared to the risk in the position.**

This a little different strategy than I used in my first Watch Me Trade book. I decided based on some feedback I received it was better to try and normalize my contracts for the purpose of this book.

Table of Contents:

Short hand used throughout the book:

BC: Buy to Close a new position.

BO: Buy to Open a new position.

C: Call Option.

CT: Contracts

GTC: Good to Cancel

P: Put Option.

SO: Sell to Open a new position.

SC: Sell to Close an open position.

Chapter 1

Iron Condors

Iron condors are a favorite of mine.

I typically trade one strategy on indexes such as RUT, SPX and NDX and another on other types of stocks. I will describe my index Iron Condor strategy first.

First of all, I prefer SPX because I have found it trades more predictable to me. I seem to run into problems more often with RUT and NDX. That is not to say I do not trade them, just that I prefer the SPX.

An iron condor is a range bound strategy consisting short calls and puts and long calls and puts. Your outlook with a iron condor is direction neutral. You enter into an iron condor with a net credit. You need the security you are trading to stay within your short calls and puts. The long calls and puts are just to reduce your risk and margin requirements, otherwise it would be a strangle.

An iron condor has an identifiable maximum profit and maximum risk when you enter the trade, that is another good thing about them. I really do not mind having a capped profit potential if the returns are where I need them. The main thing I always try to get is a capped risk.

One strategy with an iron condor is to wait for expiration and keep all your initial credit. I rarely do that, I like to decide what return I need and put in a GTC order. When it hits, I get out.

About half the time I start an iron condor as an iron condor, the rest of the time I start with at put or call credit spread and then attempt to complete the other side to end up with my condor. If I do not get the fill I want on the second part of the condor, not a problem I just trade my credit spread.

I love trading condors on the major indexes because I have found them to be consistently profitable. At the time of writing this book my Iron Condors have been profitable 82.50% of the time over the past 40 trades. My annualized return for those trades has been 45.89% of my risk.

It is important to remember that is the return of my risk, not my entire account. I never trade all (or even an a large portion) of my account in one trade and neither should you.

My average risk over those trades was about $12,000.00 per trade. My average time in a condor is about 34 days.

My Profit/Loss ratio was about .58 which is not very good. But I want to be completely honest so I am sharing it with you. The reason for that is because I did not follow my own rules (see below) on some of my trades. If I had, my Profit/Loss ratio would have been MUCH better. This is important because I want you to remember, "Have a plan and stick to your plan!"

I do have some rules I try and follow when setting up an iron condor.

1. I like the delta of my short position to be 10 or less.
2. It is better to start your condor when volatility is high. You will actually make money as the volatility goes down.
3. Need at least 49 days until expiration but prefer not more than about 62.
4. It is better if you can see clear support and/or resistance on the chart protecting your positions.

When to adjust.

1. I typically try to adjust if the delta of one of my short positions goes above 30.
2. If the price gets too close to my short options. I cannot give you exactly what that number is because it is different depending on the security and volatility.

The second type of Iron Condor strategy that I use I primarily use on stocks and EFT's. For these trades I look for the following:

1. No earnings before expiration. There are a few exceptions just be aware of the risk.
2. Trade should have about 45 to 52 days before expiration when I enter.
3. Security should have VERY liquid options. This is important when it comes to adjusting or closing the trade. I trade a lot of the same securities over and over.
4. Should have a high Implied Volatility as compared the the previous Implied Volatility on that security. This is to ensure you get a good premium and the full advantage of time decay and a drop in volatility to help you make money.
5. Trade should have high probability of success. This can be determined by using an option platform such as TD Ameritrade's ThinkorSwim or by looking at the Delta's of the options you are using as your shorts.
6. I typically try to close at 40% to 50% of max profit with at GTC order I put in right after I place the trade.

When to Adjust:

1. Typically I don't adjust these types of Iron Condors, I take much smaller risk therefore just let them play out based on the initial probability of success.
2. If I do adjust then I only adjust if I can get a credit to do so. That way I am reducing my risk.

You will see two types of condors in my trading. The traditional Iron Condor which has the same spread on the puts and the calls and a Broken Wing Iron Condor which has a different spread on either the Calls or Puts.

The main difference is on a Broken Wing Iron Condor you

can only lose money on one side of the 'Wing' of the Condor. These are a little more of a directional trade than my normal Iron Condor.

Ok, let's get started with some actual trade examples of how I trade Iron Condors.

SPX – 07/31/2018 – Iron Condor

I started this trade looking for an Iron Condor, I entered the Put side first and was filled in about a day. Next I entered an order for my Calls but … I was never able to get filled at a level I was comfortable with.

SPX was trading near all time highs and I just could not get the Call side I wanted. Therefore, this trade ended up being a Bull Put Credit Spread. I decided to leave it in the Condor section because it was meant as an Condor.

When I entered my Puts, SPX was trading at $2816.00. I sold the 9/21/18 $2620/$2595 spread for $1.25. My total risk was $11,906.25 with a credit of $593.75.

If I held to close my return would be about 4.9%. I set a GTC order to keep a 3.67% return and waited.

On 8/15 SPX had a fairly large down day. It hit $2800 but was still a LONG way away from threatening my short Put.

On 8/27 SPX spiked up to $2895 and my GTC order hit, closing me out for my target profit.

Date		EXP	Strike	Price	Ct	C/P	Cost	Balance
07/31/18	S O	09/21/18	2620	10.4	5	P	$5,196.75	$5,196.75
07/31/18	B O	09/21/18	2595	9.15	5	P	-$4,603.00	$593.75
08/27/18	B C	09/21/18	2620	2.1	5	P	-$1,053.25	-$459.50

Date		EXP	Strike	Price	Ct	C/P	Cost	Balance
08/27/18	S C	09/21/18	2595	1.85	5	P	$897.00	$437.50
							Profit of	$437.50

SPX – 08/28/18 – Iron Condor

Once the above trade closed I immediately started looking for my next Condor in SPX. Once again I started with one side of the trade only. This time because SPX was spiking up I was able to get into the Call side of the trade first.

On 8/28 with SPX at $2900.35 I got my Call spread of $3030/$3040 filled for $.60.

It took me two days to get into the Put side of the trade. I had to adjust my strikes up a few times and lower my credit but I finally got the trade filled. Did not get the fills I wanted but I still feel pretty good about the position.

On 8/30 with SPX at $2901.50 I got my Put spread of $2705/$2695 filled for $.50.

If I held to close that would be about a 11.7% return on my risk. However, I set a GTC Order to keep about one half of my initial credit.

In the end my GTC hit on 9/17 and I ended this trade with a profit of $203.95 or 5.7% on a trade that lasted 20 days. This was a pretty simple SPX Iron Condor, I wish they all ended this way.

Date		EXP	Strike	Price	Ct	C/P	Cost	Balance
08/28/18	B O	10/19/18	3040	$3.48	4	C	-$1,394.65	-$1,394.65
08/28/18	S O	10/19/18	3030	$4.08	4	C	$1,624.40	$229.75
08/30/18	S O	10/19/18	2705	$10.00	4	P	$3,997.35	$4,227.10
08/30/18	B O	10/19/18	2695	$9.50	4	P	-$3,807.60	$419.50
09/17/18	S	10/19/18	3040	$1.55	4	C	$617.35	$1,036.85

	C								
09/17/18	B C	10/19/18	3030	$1.80	4	C	-$722.65	$314.20
09/17/18	B C	10/19/18	2705	$4.70	4	P	-$1,882.65	-$1,568.45
09/17/18	S C	10/19/18	2695	$4.45	4	P	$1,772.40	$203.95
							Profit of:	$203.95

EWZ – 9/4/18 – Iron Condor

Saw a quick opportunity to get into a high probability trade on EWZ. The implied volatility looked good and the chart supported my short positions.

On 9/4 I sold the 10/19 $37 Call and purchased the $40 Call to cover it. At the same time I sold the 10/19 $27 Put and purchased the $23 Put to finish up the condor with EWZ trading at $31.36. I had a pretty good profit zone and everything worked out great when the trade hit my GTC on 9/19, just 15 days later.

I finished with a profit of $44.00 on an initial risk of $311.00 or about 14% return. EWZ was trading at $32.73 when I closed.

Date		EXP	Strike	Price	Ct	C/P	Cost	Balance
09/04/18	S O	10/19/18	$37.00	$0.54	1	C	$54.00	$54.00
09/04/18	B O	10/19/18	$40.00	$0.21	1	C	-$21.00	$33.00
09/04/18	S O	10/19/18	$27.00	$0.74	1	P	$74.00	$107.00
09/04/18	B O	10/19/18	$23.00	$0.14	1	P	-$18.00	$89.00
09/19/18	B C	10/19/18	$37.00	$0.37	1	C	-$37.00	$52.00
09/19/18	S C	10/19/18	$40.00	$0.07	1	C	$7.00	$59.00
09/19/18	B C	10/19/18	$27.00	$0.18	1	P	-$18.00	$41.00

Date		EXP	Strike	Price	Ct	C/P	Cost	Balance
09/19/18	S C	10/19/18	$23.00	$0.03	1	P	$3.00	$44.00
							Profit of:	$44.00

EWZ – 9/04/18 – Broken Wind Iron Condor

I took this trade out the same day I did the EWZ trade above. I traded it as a comparison to different strategies and risk/reward expectations.

Both trades were profitable (this time) I typically don't trade the same security with two different strategies at the same time unless it is some kind of hedge trade. I did it this time just for you and this book.

When I entered this trade on 9/4 as a Broken Wind Iron Condor I traded it so that I had no upside risk and my downside break even as at $29.03. Remember a Broken Wind Iron Condor is somewhat of a directional play as compared to a regular Iron Condor.

Everything went very well and on 9/21 my GTC order was hit and the position closed. My overall risk was $406.00 and my max profit would have been $394.00 if I held to the end, which I don't usually do. Instead I closed early for a profit of $144.00 or 35.47% over 17 days. Wish all my trades worked out this well!

Date		EXP	Strike	Price	Ct	C/P	Cost	Balance
09/04/18	S O	10/19/18	$31.00	$2.46	2	C	$492.00	$492.00
09/04/18	B O	10/19/18	$32.00	$2.00	2	C	-$400.00	$92.00
09/04/18	S O	10/19/18	$31.00	$2.28	2	P	$456.00	$548.00
09/04/18	B O	10/19/18	$27.00	$0.77	2	P	-$154.00	$394.00
09/21/18	B C	10/19/18	$31.00	$3.50	2	C	-$700.00	-$306.00
09/21/18	S C	10/19/18	$32.00	$2.78	2	C	$556.00	$250.00
09/21/18	B	10/19/18	$31.00	$0.60	2	P	-$120.00	$130.00

Date		EXP	Strike	Price	Ct	C/P	Cost	Balance
	C							
09/21/18	S C	10/19/18	$27.00	$0.07	2	P	$14.00	$144.00
							Profit of:	$144.00

DIA – 9/4/18 – Iron Condor

I started this trade with DIA trading at $259.18 and it did not go as smoothly as some of my others. On 10/3 I was considering rolling this trade out another month or closing for a small profit.

In the end I decided to hold and let the probabilities play out a little longer. DIA cooperated and pulled back and hit my updated GTC order on 10/8. I say updated because I decided to take less profit on the pull back as opposed to holding to see what happened. Perhaps I got a little lucky here or perhaps the percentages favored me.

I closed this trade for a $64.00 profit on a risk of $756.00 or 8.47% over 34 days.

Date		EXP	Strike	Price	Ct	C/P	Cost	Balance
09/04/18	B O	10/19/18	$244.00	$1.12	2	C	-$224.00	-$224.00
09/04/18	S O	10/19/18	$249.00	$1.62	2	C	$324.00	$100.00
09/04/18	S O	10/19/18	$267.00	$1.14	2	P	$228.00	$328.00
09/04/18	B O	10/19/18	$272.00	$0.42	2	P	-$84.00	$244.00
10/08/18	B C	10/19/18	$267.00	$0.85	2	C	-$170.00	$74.00
10/08/18	S C	10/19/18	$272.00	$0.15	2	C	$30.00	$104.00
10/08/18	B C	10/19/18	$249.00	$0.47	2	P	-$94.00	$10.00
10/08/18	S C	10/19/18	$244.00	$0.27	2	P	$54.00	$64.00
							Profit of:	$64.00

HD – 9/05/18 – Iron Condor

On 9/5 I decided to place an Iron Condor trade on HD. HD was trading at $204.27 with an implied volatility rank of 13, not great but I decided to go with it anyway.

When I placed the trade I had a 60.5% probability of success if I held to expiration.

I sold the 10/19 $215 Call and purchased the $220.00 Call to cover it, then sold the 10/19 $195 Put and purchased the $190 Put to finish up my Iron Condor.

On 9/25 my GTC order hit and I was able to close the trade for a profit after just 20 days. I made $39.00 on a risk of $385.00 or about 10.13%. The overall return was a little lower than I prefer but at least I made money.

Date		EXP	Strike	Price	Ct	C/P	Cost	Balance
09/05/18	S O	10/19/18	$215.00	$1.12	1	C	$112.00	$112.00
09/05/18	B O	10/19/18	$220.00	$0.53	1	C	-$53.00	$59.00
09/05/18	S O	10/19/18	$195.00	$1.50	1	P	$150.00	$209.00
09/05/18	B O	10/19/18	$190.00	$0.90	1	P	-$94.00	$115.00
09/25/18	B C	10/19/18	$215.00	$0.82	1	C	-$82.00	$33.00
09/25/18	S C	10/19/18	$220.00	$0.29	1	C	$29.00	$62.00
09/25/18	B C	10/19/18	$195.00	$0.43	1	P	-$47.00	$15.00
09/25/18	S C	10/19/18	$190.00	$0.24	1	P	$24.00	$39.00
							Profit of:	$39.00

AMAT – 9/10/18 – Broken Wing Iron Condor

On 9/10 AMAT had moved down to what I really felt would be a good support area so I decided to enter a Broken Wing Iron Condor figuring this trade would head back up.

Because I entered this trade at about a $1.43 credit, since my Calls were 1 point away that meant that if AMAT finished anywhere above $40.00 the least I would make if held to expiration was $43.00.

With AMAT trading at $39.54 I sold the 10/19 $40 Call and purchased the $41 Call to cover it. I also sold the 10/19 $39 Put and purchased the $34 Put to finish out my Broken Wing Iron Condor. My credit was $143.00 and based on my $5.00 Put spread my risk was $357.00 to the downside and none to the upside.

If we held to expiration we would want this trade to close between $39 and $40 for a max profit of $143.00 but since we always put in a GTC order I wanted to try for about a $50.00 profit at any point during this trade. Initially, this trade was showing a 67% probability of success.

Almost from the beginning this trade did not cooperate with me and was showing a loss most of the time. On 10/2 it had a pretty big up day which gave me the opportunity to close for a profit, so I took it.

I ended up with a $26.00 profit after 22 days on my risk of $357.00 which is a 7.28% return.

I closed this position with AMAT trading at $39.14.

Date		EXP	Strike	Price	Ct	C/P	Cost	Balance
09/10/18	S O	10/19/18	$40.00	$1.47	1	C	$147.00	$147.00
09/10/18	B O	10/19/18	$41.00	$1.05	1	C	-$105.00	$42.00
09/10/18	S O	10/19/18	$39.00	$1.26	1	P	$126.00	$168.00
09/10/18	B O	10/19/18	$34.00	$0.21	1	P	-$25.00	$143.00

Date		EXP	Strike	Price	Ct	C/P	Cost	Balance
10/02/18	B C	10/19/18	$40.00	$0.67	1	C	-$67.00	$76.00
10/02/18	S C	10/19/18	$41.00	$0.35	1	C	$35.00	$111.00
10/02/18	B C	10/19/18	$39.00	$0.86	1	P	-$90.00	$21.00
10/02/18	S C	10/19/18	$34.00	$0.05	1	P	$5.00	$26.00
							Profit of:	$26.00

QQQ – 9/10/18 – Iron Condor

Decided to place a QQQ trade on 9/10, really the credit I got was not all that great when I entered the trade. I was trying to stay in the market and liked the strikes I was able to get so decided to go for it.

When I entered this trade it had about a 66% chance of success if held to expiration. With QQQ trading at $181.35 I sold the 10/26 $192.50 Call and purchased the $195.00 Call to cover it. I finished out my Iron Condor by selling the $170.00 Put and purchasing the $167.50 Put.

Part of the reason my credit wasn't all that great was because I used a $2.50 spread. A larger spread would have given me a larger credit.

I was able to close this trade on 10/4 for a profit of $42.00 or about 10.50%.

Date		EXP	Strike	Price	Ct	C/P	Cost	Balance
09/10/18	S O	10/26/18	$192.50	$0.47	2	C	$94.00	$94.00
09/10/18	B O	10/26/18	$195.00	$0.33	2	C	-$46.00	$48.00
09/10/18	S O	10/26/18	$170.00	$1.55	2	P	$310.00	$358.00
09/10/18	B O	10/26/18	$167.50	$1.25	2	P	-$258.00	$100.00
10/04/18	B	10/26/18	$192.50	$0.26	2	C	-$52.00	$48.00

	C							
10/04/18	S C	10/26/18	$195.00	$0.10	2	C	$20.00	$68.00
10/04/18	B C	10/26/18	$170.00	$0.38	2	P	-$76.00	-$8.00
10/04/18	S C	10/26/18	$167.50	$0.29	2	P	$50.00	$42.00
						Profit of:	$42.00	

INTC – 9/11/18 – Broken Wing Iron Condor

Entered this trade on 9/11 with no upside risk thinking there would be more chance of a move up after a hard move down. Implied Volatility was 46 and I was showing a 64.20% probability of success.

This was a counter trend or contrarian bet that INTC would not continue down without finding buyers willing to get in at a steep discount.

The overall market made some major moves down so I moved my initial GTC order up to try and get out of this trade with as much profit as possible.

When I entered this trade I had a risk of $88.00 and a potential profit of $112.00. I closed the trade on 10/15 for a profit of $22.00 or about 25% over 34 days.

Date		EXP	Strike	Price	Ct	C/P	Cost	Balance
09/11/18	S O	10/19/18	$45.00	$1.75	1	C	$175.00	$175.00
09/11/18	B O	10/19/18	$46.00	$1.22	1	C	-$122.00	$53.00
09/11/18	S O	10/19/18	$45.00	$1.14	1	P	$114.00	$167.00
09/11/18	B O	10/19/18	$43.00	$0.55	1	P	-$55.00	$112.00
10/15/18	B C	10/19/18	$45.00	$0.72	1	C	-$72.00	$40.00

10/15/18	S C	10/19/18	$46.00	$0.28	1	C	$28.00	$68.00
10/15/18	B C	10/19/18	$45.00	$0.60	1	P	-$60.00	$8.00
10/15/18	S C	10/19/18	$43.00	$0.14	1	P	$14.00	$22.00
							Profit of:	$22.00

V – 9/13/18 – Broken Wind Iron Condor

This was part of a series of trades I did in V working different strategies to take advantage of V's run up to highs and pull back. I felt there was more downward pressure and it would be difficult for V to break to new highs over the course of this trade.

I entered this trade with V at 147.29 with no downside risk and a break even on the upside of $153.69 which would have been a new 52 week high.

The implied volatility when I entered the trade was 15.88 and I was showing a 74% chance of a successful trade if held until expiration. My risk was $390.00 and my max profit would have been $360.00 in a perfect world but I only wanted about a third of that when I set my GTC order.

I sold the 10/26 $152.50 Call while purchasing the $155.00 Call. On the Put side I sold the $150.00 Put and purchased the $149.00 Put.

On 10/8 after 25 days my GTC order was hit and I closed this trade for a $120.00 profit or 30.77%. I wish I had these types of trades everyday.

Date		EXP	Strike	Price	Ct	C/P	Cost	Balance
09/13/18	S O	10/26/18	$152.50	$1.74	3	C	$522.00	$522.00
09/13/18	B O	10/26/18	$155.00	$1.09	3	C	-$327.00	$195.00
09/13/18	S	10/26/18	$150.00	$5.00	3	P	$1,500.00	$1,695.00

Date		EXP	Strike	Price	Ct	C/P	Cost	Balance
	O							
09/13/18	B O	10/26/18	$149.00	$4.45	3	P	-$1,335.00	$360.00
10/08/18	B C	10/26/18	$152.50	$0.61	3	C	-$183.00	$177.00
10/08/18	S C	10/26/18	$155.00	$0.31	3	C	$93.00	$270.00
10/08/18	B C	10/26/18	$150.00	$6.85	3	P	-$2,055.00	-$1,785.00
10/08/18	S C	10/26/18	$149.00	$6.35	3	P	$1,905.00	$120.00
							Profit of:	$120.00

EEM – 9/14/18 – Broken Wind Iron Condor

On 9/14 EEM was trading at $41.99 and I decided to take a trade with no downside risk because if a Diagonal trade I had that was showing a loss. This was a hedge trade to protect my Diagonal to the downside.

I sold the 10/26 $42 Call and purchased the $45 Call. I sold the $42 Put and bought the $41 Put to finish out the Broken Wing Iron Condor. My max loss would be $338 and my break even to the upside was $43.31.

Just looking at this on its own merit I had a 68.27% probability of success if held to the expiration.

I closed this trade on 10/12 for a profit of $64.00 which went to offset some of my open loss on the Diagonal. This was a profit of 18.93% over 28 days.

Date		EXP	Strike	Price	Ct	C/P	Cost	Balance
09/14/18	S O	10/26/18	$42.00	$1.14	2	C	$228.00	$228.00
09/14/18	B O	10/26/18	$45.00	$0.18	2	C	-$36.00	$192.00
09/14/18	S O	10/26/18	$42.00	$1.01	2	P	$202.00	$394.00

09/14/18	B O	10/26/18	$41.00	$0.66	2	P	-$140.00	$254.00
10/12/18	B C	10/26/18	$42.00	$0.15	2	C	-$30.00	$224.00
10/12/18	S C	10/26/18	$45.00	$0.01	2	C	$2.00	$226.00
10/12/18	B C	10/26/18	$42.00	$1.98	2	P	-$396.00	-$170.00
10/12/18	S C	10/26/18	$41.00	$1.21	2	P	$234.00	$64.00
							Profit of:	$64.00

SPX – 9/17/18 – Iron Condor

This was one of my most difficult trades of the year. It was an SPX Iron Condor which I have pretty strict rules for trading but it was moving up and then down so fast that I struggled to trade my rules.

On 9/17 with SPX trading at $2902.00 I entered an Iron Condor expecting easy profits like I had seen throughout the year trading these. I started the trade by selling the $3020.00 Call and buying the $3035.00 Call to cover while selling the $2675.00 Put and buy the $2660.00 Put to cover it.

On 9/20 SPX spiked up to $2932.00 putting my short Call delta at 20, I try to adjust around 30.

On 10/3 SPX was up to $2937.39 but my short Call delta had dropped a little to 18 as the market was slowing down and time had passed. I love time decay on these.

By 10/11 SPX had dropped from $2937.39 to $2771.00, my Calls were fine now but my short Put was in trouble with a delta of 28 which increased to 31 during that day. Time to look for an adjustment.

On 10/12 I was able to roll my Puts from from 11/16 to 12/7 and from 2675/2660 to 2650/2630. I increased the spread from 15 to 20 which increased my risk for a net credit which was nice, except for the increased risk! But at least I managed to move the short Put down from

2675 to 2650.

On 10/23 SPX moved against me again down to $2700.00. I rolled my Calls down 100 points and increased their spread from 15 to 20 to match my calls to bring in a credit in order to adjust my Puts again!

I then rolled my Puts down another 50 points from 2650/2630 to 2600/2580 and my expiration from 12/7 to 12/14. I was still able to bring in a net credit from my 10/23 rolls.

On 10/25 SPX spiked down yet again to $2648.00, my short Put delta spiked up to 33 (over my 30 adjustment level). However, because I had moved down twice already I really felt the market might cooperate and move up for me. By the end of the day the market had bounced up to $2686.00 and my short Put delta was now right at 30.0

On 10/26 SPX moved down to $2640.00 and I decided to move the Puts down again and from 12/14 to 12/21 from 2600/2580 to 2570/2550. Surely this would be enough! I kept my Calls where they were because I still had a credit on this trade and was afraid it would make a rapid move up.

On 11/8 SPX spiked up to $2811.00 now and my Calls were moving toward a 30 delta on my short Call.

On 11/18 SPX had begun to pull back. I decided to roll my Call out so they would be on the same expiration as my Puts (makes closing easier) but did not roll them up. I rolled my Calls from 12/14 to 12/21 expiration.

On 11/20 SPX had dropped big over the past couple of days and my short Put delta was at 33. I decided to wait and see because of how much I had moved down already. I really felt the market was WAY oversold and there just could not be that much downward pressure left.

On 11/26 my GTC order FINALLY hit and I closed at about break even. Remember, once I make a single adjustment I move my GTC to break even to just get out of the trade as soon as possible.

I ended up with a $24.00 profit on a risk of $5001.00 or about 0.48% over 70 days. Of course, the profit here is not what is important. What is important is that I kept from losing money and came very close to following my trading rules.

When my trade finally closed SPX was at $2673.00.

Date		EXP	Strike	Price	Ct	C/P	Cost	Balance
09/17/18	SO	11/16/18	$3,020.00	$5.24	3	C	$1,572.00	$1,572.00
09/17/18	BO	11/16/18	$3,035.00	$3.97	3	C	-$1,191.00	$381.00
09/17/18	SO	11/16/18	$2,675.00	$10.74	3	P	$3,222.00	$3,603.00
09/17/18	BO	11/16/18	$2,660.00	$9.96	3	P	-$3,000.00	$603.00
10/12/18	BC	11/16/18	$2,675.00	$34.96	3	P	-$10,494.00	-$9,891.00
10/12/18	SC	11/16/18	$2,660.00	$31.69	3	P	$9,507.00	-$384.00
10/12/18	SO	12/07/18	$2,650.00	$39.99	3	P	$11,997.00	$11,613.00
10/12/18	BO	12/07/18	$2,630.00	$36.07	3	P	-$10,827.00	$786.00
10/12/18	BC	11/16/18	$3,020.00	$0.80	3	C	-$246.00	$540.00
10/12/18	SC	11/16/18	$3,035.00	$0.65	3	C	$195.00	$735.00
10/12/18	SO	12/07/18	$2,980.00	$3.50	3	C	$1,050.00	$1,785.00
10/12/18	BO	12/07/18	$3,000.00	$2.60	3	C	-$786.00	$999.00
10/23/18	BC	12/07/18	$2,980.00	$1.03	3	C	-$315.00	$684.00
10/23/18	SC	12/07/18	$3,000.00	$0.73	3	C	$219.00	$903.00
10/23/18	SO	12/14/18	$2,880.00	$7.20	3	C	$2,160.00	$3,063.00
10/23/18	BO	12/14/18	$2,900.00	$5.20	3	C	-$1,566.00	$1,497.00

10/23/18	B C	12/07/18	$2,650.00	$56.27	3	P	-$16,887.00	-$15,390.00
10/23/18	S C	12/07/18	$2,630.00	$50.54	3	P	$15,162.00	-$228.00
10/23/18	S O	12/14/18	$2,600.00	$47.29	3	P	$14,187.00	$13,959.00
10/23/18	B O	12/14/18	$2,580.00	$42.86	3	P	-$12,864.00	$1,095.00
10/26/18	B C	12/14/18	$2,600.00	$55.65	3	P	-$16,701.00	-$15,606.00
10/26/18	S C	12/14/18	$2,580.00	$50.05	3	P	$15,015.00	-$591.00
10/26/18	S O	12/21/18	$2,570.00	$52.05	3	P	$15,615.00	$15,024.00
10/26/18	B O	12/21/18	$2,550.00	$47.20	3	P	-$14,166.00	$858.00
11/18/18	B C	12/14/18	$2,880.00	$16.26	3	C	-$4,878.00	-$4,020.00
11/18/18	S C	12/14/18	$2,900.00	$10.89	3	C	$3,267.00	-$753.00
11/18/18	S O	12/21/18	$2,880.00	$21.19	3	C	$6,537.00	$5,604.00
11/18/18	B O	12/21/18	$2,900.00	$15.02	3	C	-$4,518.00	$1,086.00
11/26/18	B C	12/21/18	$2,880.00	$1.10	3	C	-$330.00	$756.00
11/26/18	S C	12/21/18	$2,900.00	$0.75	3	C	$225.00	$981.00
11/26/18	B C	12/21/18	$2,570.00	$17.85	3	P	-$5,355.00	-$4,374.00
11/26/18	S C	12/21/18	$2,550.00	$14.70	3	P	$4,422.00	$24.00
							Profit of:	$24.00

PBR – 09/20/18 – Iron Condor

On 9/20 we decided to place an Iron Condor in PBR with its Implied Volatility at 63.04. Our initial trade probability was 75.67% which was better than normal for these types of trades, so we figured what could go wrong?

With PBR at $11.29 we sold the 11/2/18 $13.50 Call and purchased the $14.50 Call. We then sold the $9.00 Put and purchased the $8.00 Put to enter the trade with a total credit of $.36. We did increased contracts because the spread was only $1.00. In retrospect this was not a good trade, so you won't see this one again.

On 10/24 PBR was trading at $15.60 and we were almost at max loss on this trade so we started seeing if we could find a roll for a credit. We got lucky and did.

We rolled out from 11/2/18 to 11/30/18 selling time. We were also able to roll up our calls from 13.50/14.50 to 14.00/15.00 increasing our chance of success.

On 11/30 (expiration day) we managed to close this trade with PBR trading at $14.27 for a small profit.

After 71 days we closed with a profit of $24.00 or 9.3% on our initial risk of $256.00

Date		EXP	Strike	Price	Ct	C/P	Cost	Balance
09/20/18	B O	11/02/18	$8.00	$0.14	4	P	-$56.00	-$56.00
09/20/18	S O	11/02/18	$9.00	$0.32	4	P	$128.00	$72.00
09/20/18	S O	11/02/18	$13.50	$0.45	4	C	$180.00	$252.00
09/20/18	B O	11/02/18	$14.50	$0.27	4	C	-$108.00	$144.00
10/24/18	B C	11/02/18	$13.50	$2.27	4	C	-$908.00	-$764.00
10/24/18	S C	11/02/18	$14.50	$1.42	4	C	$568.00	-$196.00
10/24/18	B C	11/02/18	$9.00	$0.01	4	P	-$4.00	-$200.00
10/24/18	S C	11/02/18	$8.00	$0.00	4	P	$0.00	-$200.00
10/24/18	S	11/30/18	$14.00	$2.12	4	C	$848.00	$648.00

	O							
10/24/18	B O	11/30/18	$15.00	$1.44	4	C	-$576.00	$72.00
10/24/18	S O	11/30/18	$14.00	$0.45	4	P	$180.00	$252.00
10/24/18	B O	11/30/18	$13.00	$0.26	4	P	-$104.00	$148.00
11/30/18	B C	11/30/18	$14.00	$0.29	4	C	-$116.00	$32.00
11/30/18	S C	11/30/18	$15.00	$0.01	4	C	$4.00	$36.00
11/30/18	B C	11/30/18	$14.00	$0.04	4	P	-$16.00	$20.00
11/30/18	S C	11/30/18	$13.00	$0.01	4	P	$4.00	$24.00
							Profit of:	$24.00

XOP – 9/24/18 – Broken Wing Iron Condor

XOP was trading at $43.22 and I thought a move down or a sideways move was the most likely outcome over the next month or so. I entered this trade with no downside risk and an upside break even of $45.57.

When I entered this one Implied Volatility was at 13.40 and moving down which is good. It was also showing a 71.7% probability of success.

I sold the 11/16 $44 Call and purchased the $48 Call. I sold the $44 Put and bought the $43 Put. My max risk was $486.00 with a max profit potential of $306.00. I set a GTC order to keep about $80.00 of the potential.

On 10/11 XOP was down big at $41.16 and my trade was showing a profit. Probability of success is now 82%.

On 10/18 my GTC order hit as XOP was bouncing off of a bottom and moving back up.

I closed for a profit of $78.00 or 16.05% over 24 days.

Date		EXP	Strike	Price	Ct	C/P	Cost	Balance
09/24/18	S O	11/16/18	$44.00	$1.37	2	C	$274.00	$274.00
09/24/18	B O	11/16/18	$48.00	$0.29	2	C	-$58.00	$216.00
09/24/18	S O	11/16/18	$44.00	$2.05	2	P.	$410.00	$626.00
09/24/18	B O	11/16/18	$43.00	$1.56	2	P	-$320.00	$306.00
10/18/18	B C	11/16/18	$44.00	$0.32	2	C	-$64.00	$242.00
10/18/18	S C	11/16/18	$48.00	$0.07	2	C	$14.00	$256.00
10/18/18	B C	11/16/18	$44.00	$3.74	2	P	-$748.00	-$492.00
10/18/18	S C	11/16/18	$43.00	$2.89	2	P	$570.00	$78.00
							Profit of:	$78.00

IYR – 09/24/18 – Broken Wing Condor

I decided to place a Broken Wing Condor in IYR after a move down with no risk to the upside. I felt it had its run down and now was due for a rebound. Turns out I was wrong, that is the problem with trying to pick a direction.

With IYR trading at $80.71 I sold the 11/16 $80 Call and purchased the $81 Call. I sold the $80 Put and purchased the $76 Put to cover my long Put. My risk was about $500.00 with a potential max profit of $292.00 if held to expiration and the security finished at the optimal price of $80.11. Implied volatility was at 28.67 but appeared to be rising, if I was right about the price moving back up then the implied volatility would start to go down which is what I would prefer.

As I stated above, turns out I was wrong and the security starting a move up. I had varying degrees of loss for almost the entire trade. On 11/5 with a move up in IYR I decided to take advantage of the move and close the position with IYR trading at $78.71.

I ended up with a loss of $52.00 or about 10.4%. Based on my rules I probably should have just let this trade play out, but sometimes I don't follow my own rules. Trading is a little science and a little art.

The best reason I can give you for why I did not follow my own rules is two part. One, this trade had been at a much greater loss and had not preformed well from the beginning. Two, I had been in this trade for 42 days which is a long time for these. It was time to close.

Date		EXP	Strike	Price	Ct	C/P	Cost	Balance
09/24/18	S O	11/16/18	$80.00	$1.60	2	C	$320.00	$320.00
09/24/18	B O	11/16/18	$81.00	$1.04	2	C	-$208.00	$112.00
09/24/18	S O	11/16/18	$80.00	$1.45	2	P	$290.00	$402.00
09/24/18	B O	11/16/18	$76.00	$0.51	2	P	-$110.00	$292.00
11/05/18	B C	11/16/18	$80.00	$0.49	2	C	-$98.00	$194.00
11/05/18	S C	11/16/18	$81.00	$0.22	2	C	$44.00	$238.00
11/05/18	B C	11/16/18	$80.00	$1.76	2	P	-$352.00	-$114.00
11/05/18	S C	11/16/18	$76.00	$0.35	2	P	$62.00	-$52.00
							Profit of:	-$52.00

TLT – 09/25/18 – Broken Wing Iron Condor

I got in a little bit of a habit of placing these Broken Wing Iron Condors during this time period. Great if you are expecting the market to move a certain direction, but don't over do them. If the market suddenly changes on you and you are playing the directional game you will get burned fast.

On 9/25 I entered this trade with no upside risk. My break even was at $133.74, Implied Volatility was at 24.8 and looked to be rising. It showed an almost 73% probability of success; I set my GTC to keep about half of my potential profit.

Just 2 days later my GTC order hit and I closed the trade for a $59.00 profit or about 15.69%. Yes, and in just 2 DAYS!

Date		EXP	Strike	Price	Ct	C/P	Cost	Balance
09/25/18	S O	11/16/18	$117.00	$1.38	1	C	$138.00	$138.00
09/25/18	B O	11/16/18	$118.00	$0.97	1	C	-$97.00	$41.00
09/25/18	S O	11/16/18	$115.00	$1.09	1	P	$109.00	$150.00
09/25/18	B O	11/16/18	$110.00	$0.22	1	P	-$26.00	$124.00
9/27/18	B C	11/16/18	$117.00	$1.55	1	C	-$155.00	-$31.00
09/27/18	S C	11/16/18	$118.00	$1.35	1	C	$135.00	$104.00
09/27/18	B C	11/16/18	$115.00	$0.63	1	P	-$63.00	$41.00
09/27/18	S C	11/16/18	$110.00	$0.22	1	P	$22.00	$59.00
							Profit of:	$59.00

CRM – 9/28/18 – Iron Condor

I have always struggling trading CRM, not sure why I keep trying. The return here looked pretty good, I guess that is one reason I keep trying to trade it.

On 9/28 I entered into a 11/16 Iron Condor selling the $175 Call and purchasing the $180 Call. I sold the $150 Put and purchased the $145 Put for a total of a $1.30 credit on a $3.70 risk per contract.

CRM had an implied volatility of 28.6 when I started the trade and a probability of success of 62.68%. My break even points were at $148.68 and $176.28. CRM was trading at $159.44 when I started the trade.

On 11/8 CRM was trading at $142.47 about half way between my short and long Puts. I decided to try and roll the position out to 12/21 if I could do it for a credit. I was lucky (or at least I thought I was) and was able to roll the entire position to 12/21 keeping the same strikes.

By 12/17 CRM was trading at $127.97, well below both my short and long Put, I had known for some time I had no hope of rolling the position so I was just waiting until 12/21 to close everything. Unfortunately someone decided to assign me my short Put and I ended up owning the shares. I promptly sold the shares and my remaining long Put to close that side of the trade. I just let the Calls expire worthless, the weren't worth the commissions to close.

I took a 100% loss of $370.00 on this trade that lasted 81 days.

Date		EXP	Strike	Price	Ct	C/P	Cost	Balance
09/28/18	S O	11/16/18	$175.00	$1.07	1	C	$107.00	$107.00
09/28/18	B O	11/16/18	$180.00	$0.60	1	C	-$62.00	$45.00
09/28/18	S O	11/16/18	$150.00	$2.18	1	P	$218.00	$263.00
09/28/18	B O	11/16/18	$145.00	$1.35	1	P	-$137.00	$126.00
11/05/18	B C	11/16/18	$175.00	$0.03	1	C	-$3.00	$123.00
11/05/18	S C	11/16/18	$180.00	$0.02	1	C	$2.00	$125.00
11/05/18	S O	12/21/18	$165.00	$0.68	1	C	$68.00	$193.00
11/05/18	B O	12/21/18	$170.00	$0.39	1	C	-$43.00	$150.00
11/05/18	B C	12/21/18	$150.00	$7.80	1	P	-$780.00	-$630.00
11/05/18	S C	12/21/18	$145.00	$3.85	1	P	$385.00	-$245.00
11/05/18	S	12/21/18	$155.00	$14.45	1	P	$1,445.00	$1,200.00

Date		EXP	Strike	Price	Ct	C/P	Cost	Balance
	O							
11/05/18	B O	12/21/18	$150.00	$10.65	1	P	-$1,069.00	$131.00
12/17/18		Put	Assigned		100		-$15,500.00	-$15,369.00
12/18/18	S C	STC		$18.65	1	P	$1,865.00	-$13,504.00
12/18/18	S E	Sell	Shares	$131.34	100		$13,134.00	-$370.00
							Loss of:	-$370.00

EWZ – 9/28/18 – Iron Condor

Looking to stay active I decided on an Iron Condor in EWZ on 9/28. Implied Volatility was at 79 and coming down from 100 so there was good premium still to be had.

With EWZ trading at $34.14 I sold the 11/16 $40 Call and purchased the $43 Call. I also sold the $29 Put and purchased the $26 Put to finish out my Iron Condor.

My break even was $28.06 and $40.94 which I felt pretty good about going into the trade. I set my GTC order at about 50% of my potential $180.00 maximum gain with a risk of $412.00.

EWZ had been down when I entered the trade and made a larger move to the upside than I felt it would. I had been in this trade a long time on 11/8 so I decided to get out of it instead of letting the odds play out for a small profit. Might have been alright to have stayed in but with expiration closing in and because of the length of the trade I decided to close.

On 11/8 with EWZ at $39.91 I closed the trade for a profit of $10.00 or about 2.43% over 41 days. Not my best trade for sure but, I did not lose any money.

Date		EXP	Strike	Price	Ct	C/P	Cost	Balance
09/28/18	S O	11/16/18	$40.00	$0.63	2	C	$126.00	$126.00

09/28/18	B O	11/16/18	$43.00	$0.19	2	C	-$42.00	$84.00
09/28/18	S O	11/16/18	$29.00	$0.77	2	P	$154.00	$238.00
09/28/18	B O	11/16/18	$26.00	$0.27	2	P	-$58.00	$180.00
11/8/18	B C	11/16/18	$40.00	$0.86	2	C	-$172.00	$8.00
11/08/18	S C	11/16/18	$43.00	$0.05	2	C	$10.00	$18.00
11/08/18	B C	11/16/18	$29.00	$0.01	2	P	-$9.00	$9.00
11/08/18	S C	11/16/18	$26.00	$0.01	2	P	$1.00	$10.00
							Profit of:	$10.00

NKE – 10/2/18 – Iron Condor

NKE had a big earnings Implied Volatility drop after earnings but still looked pretty good for an Iron Condor. I could have gotten more premium trading before earnings but there is a huge risk doing that, which is why you get more premium.

On 10/2 I sold the 11/16 $87.50 Call and purchased the $92.50 Call to cover. I also sold the $80.00 Put, purchasing the $75.00 Put to cover with NKE trading at $83.15. I was taking a little more risk to the downside based on the Delta of the short Put but felt it would work out.

The trade did not go well as NKE continued to fall. On 11/9 I found myself with a negative trade that I either needed to roll or close for a loss. I was going on a trip and had not planned to hold any trades on the 11/16 expiration since I would be gone. So … here I was.

On 11/14 with NKE trading at $75.20 I finally decided to close for a loss because I could not find a roll that I could get for a credit.

I closed after 43 days for a loss of $268.00 on an initial risk of $358.00 or 74.86%

Date		EXP	Strike	Price	Ct	C/P	Cost	Balance
10/2/18	S O	11/16/18	$87.50	$0.96	1	C	$96.00	$96.00
10/02/18	B O	11/16/18	$92.50	$0.26	1	C	-$26.00	$70.00
10/02/18	S O	11/16/18	$80.00	$1.00	1	P	$100.00	$170.00
10/02/18	B O	11/16/18	$75.00	$0.28	1	P	-$32.00	$138.00
11/14/18	B C	11/16/18	$87.50	$0.06	1	C	-$6.00	$132.00
11/14/18	S C	11/16/18	$92.50	$0.05	1	C	$5.00	$137.00
11/14/18	B C	11/16/18	$80.00	$4.04	1	P	-$404.00	-$267.00
11/14/18	S C	11/16/18	$75.00	$0.05	1	P	-$1.00	-$268.00
							Loss of:	-$268.00

TLT – 10/2/18 – Broken Wing Iron Condor

I started this trade with TLT trading at $116.98 and took a no upside risk trade using the Broken Wing Iron Condor strategy. TLT however did not cooperate.

On 10/2 I sold the 11/16 $115 Call and purchased the $116 Call. I also sold the $115 Put and purchased the $110 Put to cover. I started out with a credit of $124.00 (also max profit) on a risk of $372.00 and set my usual GTC order.

On 11/8 TLT was trading at $112.64 so I started looking for an opportunity to roll the trade out a couple of more weeks from 11/16 to 11/30 expiration. I was able to find a credit trade that let me keep the same strikes and get about 2 more weeks for the trade to move to profitability.

One thing I typically do when I have to roll a Condor is set my GTC at break even to just get out of the trade. If I am having to defend, things have obviously gone wrong so I usually prefer to close as soon as possible and move on to another trade.

On 11/20 after 49 total days my break even GTC order hit and I was able to get out of the trade for a very small profit of $5.00 or 1.34% on my initial $372.00 risk.

Date		EXP	Strike	Price	Ct	C/P	Cost	Balance
10/2/18	S O	11/16/18	$115.00	$2.86	1	C	$286.00	$286.00
10/02/18	B O	11/16/18	$116.00	$2.16	1	C	-$216.00	$70.00
10/02/18	S O	11/16/18	$115.00	$0.71	1	P	$71.00	$141.00
10/02/18	B O	11/16/18	$110.00	$0.13	1	P	-$17.00	$124.00
11/08/18	B C	11/16/18	$115.00	$2.37	1	P	-$237.00	-$113.00
11/08/18	S C	11/16/18	$110.00	$0.06	1	P	$6.00	-$107.00
11/08/18	S O	11/30/18	$115.00	$2.48	1	P	$248.00	$141.00
11/08/18	B O	11/30/18	$110.00	$0.21	1	P	-$25.00	$116.00
11/08/18	B C	11/16/18	$115.00	$0.07	1	C	-$7.00	$109.00
11/08/18	S C	11/16/18	$116.00	$0.03	1	C	$3.00	$112.00
11/08/18	S O	11/30/18	$115.00	$0.25	1	C	$25.00	$137.00
11/08/18	B O	11/30/18	$116.00	$0.14	1	C	-$18.00	$119.00
11/20/18	B C	11/30/18	$115.00	$0.96	1	C	-$96.00	$23.00
11/20/18	S C	11/30/18	$116.00	$0.48	1	C	$48.00	$71.00
11/20/18	B C	11/30/18	$115.00	$0.66	1	P	-$70.00	$1.00
11/20/18	S C	11/30/18	$110.00	$0.04	1	P	$4.00	$5.00
							Profit of:	$5.00

FXE – 10/3/18 – Broken Wing Iron Condor

When I can find opportunities I like to trade FXE because it trends well. Finding premium can be a challenge, however.

On 10/3 with FXE trading at $110.26 and Implied Volatility at 54.75 I was able to get into a Broken Wind Iron Condor with no upside risk and a probability of success of about 73.26%. My breakeven on the down side was at $108.70.

I sold the 11/16 $110 Call and purchased the $111 Call while selling the $110 Put and buying the $106 Put to cover it for a credit of $1.28. My risk was $272.00 to the downside, and $0.00 to the upside. I put in a GTC order for $.62 and waited.

FXE did not cooperate with my great plans to make money. It moved down consistently showing losses on the trade. On 11/8 I got a spike up so after 36 days I decided to close the trade for small profit.

I made $18.00 on my $272.00 risk or about 6.62%.

Date		EXP	Strike	Price	Ct	C/P	Cost	Balance
10/03/18	S O	11/16/18	$110.00	$1.44	1	C	$144.00	$144.00
10/03/18	B O	11/16/18	$111.00	$0.93	1	C	-$93.00	$51.00
10/03/18	S O	11/16/18	$110.00	$0.93	1	P	$93.00	$144.00
10/03/18	B O	11/16/18	$106.00	$0.16	1	P	-$20.00	$124.00
11/8/18	B C	11/16/18	$110.00	$0.25	1	C	-$25.00	$99.00
11/08/18	S C	11/16/18	$111.00	$0.05	1	C	$5.00	$104.00
11/08/18	B C	11/16/18	$110.00	$0.83	1	P	-$83.00	$21.00
11/08/18	S C	11/16/18	$106.00	$0.01	1	P	-$3.00	$22.00

						Profit of:	$18.00

COST – 10/8/18 – Iron Condor

I liked the price action on COST and was able to get a pretty good premium (or at least I initially though so) with Implied Volatility at 34.04 so I decided to go with an Iron Condor.

On 10/8 with COST trading at 223.27 I sold the 11/16 $240 Call and purchased the $250 Call. I also sold the $210 Put and purchased the $200 Put.

Remember above when I said I 'thought' I got a pretty good premium. Well, I forgot to take into account that the spread was $10.00 wide on this one. In actuality this was not a great trade for the risk.

My break even was $208.55 and $241.44 and I had a 68.68% chance of success.

On 11/12 after 39 days my GTC was hit and the trade closed for a $65.00 profit. This was a return of 7.56% because my risk was $860.00, this is what I meant by not really as good of a trade as I thought.

Date		EXP	Strike	Price	Ct	C/P	Cost	Balance
10/08/18	S O	11/16/18	$240.00	$0.77	1	C	$77.00	$77.00
10/08/18	B O	11/16/18	$250.00	$0.25	1	C	-$25.00	$52.00
10/08/18	S O	11/16/18	$210.00	$1.61	1	P	$161.00	$213.00
10/08/18	B O	11/16/18	$200.00	$0.69	1	P	-$73.00	$140.00
11/12/18	B C	11/16/18	$240.00	$0.68	1	C	-$68.00	$72.00
11/12/18	S C	11/16/18	$250.00	$0.04	1	C	$4.00	$76.00
11/12/18	B C	11/16/18	$210.00	$0.11	1	P	-$11.00	$65.00

11/12/18	SC	11/16/18	$200.00	$0.04	1	P	$0.00	$65.00
							Profit of:	$65.00

WMT – 10/12/18 Iron Condor

Normally you can count on WMT to trade in a relatively predictable manner, but not always which is what I ran into on this trade.

On 10/12 with WMT trading at $94.52 I decided to place an Iron Condor trade. I sold the 11/16 $100 Call and purchased the $105 Call. I completed the Iron Condor by selling the $85 Put and covering it with the $80 Put.

WMT had an Implied Volatility of 69.49 when I started the trade which was pretty high for WMT. My probability of success was 62.49% when I started the trade.

On 11/9 WMT was trading at $105.52 which put both my short and long Call in the money and me at a loss. I started working on a roll out for a couple of more weeks provided I could do it for a credit. After a lot of playing around with weeks and strikes I was finally able to roll out the position using the same strike to the 11/30 expiration.

Since I had the adjust the trade I moved my GTC order to break even to just close the trade and move on.

On 11/15 my GTC finally hit and I closed the trade for $1.00 or .27% over 34 days. WMT had moved back to $99.54 which enabled me to close. This time the probabilities with a little help from a roll made the trade work.

Ironically, if I had just waited to the 11/16 expiration instead of trying to roll this trade would have hit my initial GTC order and I would have made closer to 11% on this trade. Oh well, sometimes trading works out that way. You think you are doing the right thing but make it worse. Sometimes it is just better to let these types of Iron Condors play out win or lose.

Date		EXP	Strike	Price	Ct	C/P	Cost	Balance
10/12/18	S O	11/16/18	$100.00	$1.37	1	C	$137.00	$137.00
10/12/18	B O	11/16/18	$105.00	$0.48	1	C	-$48.00	$89.00
10/12/18	S O	11/16/18	$85.00	$0.71	1	P	$71.00	$160.00
10/12/18	B O	11/16/18	$80.00	$0.30	1	P	-$34.00	$126.00
11/09/18	B C	11/16/18	$100.00	$6.29	1	C	-$629.00	-$503.00
11/09/18	S C	11/16/18	$105.00	$2.75	1	C	$275.00	-$228.00
11/09/18	S O	11/30/18	$100.00	$6.61	1	C	$661.00	$433.00
11/09/18	B O	11/30/18	$105.00	$3.12	1	C	-$316.00	$117.00
11/13/18	B C	11/16/18	$85.00	$0.35	1	P	-$35.00	$82.00
11/13/18	S C	11/16/18	$80.00	$0.40	1	P	$40.00	$122.00
11/13/18	S O	11/30/18	$90.00	$0.41	1	P	$41.00	$163.00
11/13/18	B O	11/30/18	$85.00	$0.36	1	P	-$40.00	$123.00
11/15/18	B C	11/30/18	$100.00	$1.29	1	C	-$129.00	-$6.00
11/15/18	S C	11/30/18	$105.00	$0.19	1	C	$19.00	$13.00
11/15/18	B C	11/30/18	$90.00	$0.14	1	P	-$18.00	-$5.00
11/15/18	S C	11/30/18	$85.00	$0.06	1	P	$6.00	$1.00
							Profit of:	$1.00

EEM – 10/12/18 – Iron Condor

This was a hedge trade I had on a Diagonal that was losing money. I wanted to try and take advantage of EEM moving into a sideways range after a move down and use that premium to help my Diagonal.

I entered this Iron Condor with EEM trading at 40.14, an Implied Volatility of 62.08 and a probability of success of 67.40% which meant this was a good Iron Condor even if there was no hedge. Sometimes I will skew my hedge Iron Condor's to protect my hedge, this trade however could have been traded on its own merit.

On 10/12 I sold the 11/16 $42 Call and purchased the $45 Call. I sold the $37 Put and purchased the $34 Put to cover. This gave me a $3.00 spread and a total risk of $490.00 with a potential profit of $110.00. My break even prices were $36.41 and $42.59.

On 11/1 after 20 days my GTC order hit and I closed this trade for a profit of $52.00 or about 10.61%. Not as good as I prefer but as a hedge it was fine.

Date		EXP	Strike	Price	Ct	C/P	Cost	Balance
10/12/18	S O	11/16/18	$42.00	$0.44	2	C	$88.00	$88.00
10/12/18	B O	11/16/18	$45.00	$0.05	2	C	-$10.00	$78.00
10/12/18	S O	11/16/18	$37.00	$0.29	2	P	$58.00	$136.00
10/12/18	B O	11/16/18	$34.00	$0.09	2	P	-$26.00	$110.00
11/11/18	B C	11/16/18	$42.00	$0.10	2	C	-$20.00	$90.00
11/11/18	S C	11/16/18	$45.00	$0.01	2	C	$2.00	$92.00
11/11/18	B C	11/16/18	$37.00	$0.17	2	P	-$42.00	$50.00
11/11/18	S C	11/16/18	$34.00	$0.01	2	P	$2.00	$52.00
							Profit of:	$52.00

MU – 10/18/18 – Broken Wing Iron Condor

I trade MU from time to time so I keep and eye on its price action. I felt it had pulled back a little and now was more likely to continue an upward move or at the very least stay in a range.

With MU trading at $41.68 I decided to enter a Broken Wing Iron Condor with no upside risk. The implied volatility was at 23.24 which actually went up over the trade instead of down. My probably of success was 64.15% if held to expiration, which of course I was not going to do.

On 11/8 my GTC order was hit and I closed the order for a $77.00 profit or about 15.28% on a $504.00 risk. My max profit was $296.00 if everything worked out perfect.

Date		EXP	Strike	Price	Ct	C/P	Cost	Balance
10/18/18	S O	11/16/18	$42.00	$1.84	2	C	$368.00	$368.00
10/18/18	B O	11/16/18	$43.00	$1.40	2	C	-$280.00	$88.00
10/18/18	S O	11/16/18	$41.00	$1.55	2	P	$310.00	$398.00
10/18/18	B O	11/16/18	$37.00	$0.47	2	P	-$102.00	$296.00
11/08/18	B C	11/16/18	$42.00	$0.69	2	C	-$138.00	$158.00
11/08/18	S C	11/16/18	$43.00	$0.36	2	C	$72.00	$230.00
11/08/18	B C	11/16/18	$41.00	$0.86	2	P	-$172.00	$58.00
11/08/18	S C	11/16/18	$37.00	$0.09	2	P	$19.00	$77.00
							Profit of:	$77.00

XOP – 10/18/18 – Iron Condor

XOP is another security I like to trade because it is somewhat predictable. That is, unless it is not. This trade went bad pretty quickly, just bad luck really, I got in at the worst time and once it started to move against me I decided to hold and play the probabilities. They did not work out this time.

On 10/18 with XOP trading at $40.38 I entered into an Iron Condor expecting XOP to say within a range. I sold the 11/23 $44 Call and purchased the $47 Call. I sold the $38 Put and purchased the $35 Put.

Implied Volatility was at 43.03 and looked to be going down which was another plus for me on this trade. My initial probability for success was 62.56%.

As I said, this trade just did not work out. On 11/19 with XOP trading below my short AND long Puts I was assigned on my short Put. Being this far in the money there was really no sense in even looking for a roll, especially since I had already been assigned. I sold my assigned long stock position and sold my long Put to close out the trade.

I just let my Calls expire, not sense paying commissions to close them since they were so far out of the money.

I ended up with a loss of $230.00 on a risk of about $230.00 or 100%. I was in this trade for 36 days.

Date		EXP	Strike	Price	Ct	C/P	Cost	Balance
10/18/18	S O	11/23/18	$44.00	$0.36	1	C	$36.00	$36.00
10/18/18	B O	11/23/18	$47.00	$0.06	1	C	-$6.00	$30.00
10/18/18	S O	11/23/18	$38.00	$0.66	1	P	$66.00	$96.00
10/18/18	B O	11/23/18	$35.00	$0.27	1	P	-$27.00	$69.00
11/19/18	A S	Assigned			200		-$3,800.00	-$3,731.00
11/20/18		Sold	Shares	$32.90	200		$3,298.00	-$433.00
11/20/18		11/23/18	$35.00	$2.04			$203.00	-$203.00
							Loss of:	-$230.00

V – 10/25/18 – Iron Condor

This was another hedge trade that I did to offset some losses I was showing on a Diagonal I had on.

On 10/25 with V trading at $139.69 I placed an Iron Condor to take advantage of V if it stayed range bound as part of my Diagonal hedge. I sold the 11/30 $145 Call and covered it with the $149 Call. I sold the $124 Put and covered it with the $120 Put for a credit of $1.25.

My GTC order was hit on 11/19 after 25 days giving me a profit of $61.00 on a risk of $279.00 or 21.86% which was a very good return. When I entered the trade V had an Implied Volatility of 42.1 which enabled me to get a good premium. Because this was a hedge I also picked my short Call a little closer than normal. Still this traded started out with a 62.9% chance of success.

Date		EXP	Strike	Price	Ct	C/P	Cost	Balance
10/25/18	S O	11/30/18	$145.00	$1.88	1	C	$188.00	$188.00
10/25/18	B O	11/30/18	$149.00	$0.82	1	C	-$82.00	$106.00
10/25/18	S O	11/30/18	$124.00	$0.85	1	P	$85.00	$191.00
10/25/18	B O	11/30/18	$120.00	$0.66	1	P	-$70.00	$121.00
11/19/18	B C	11/30/18	$145.00	$0.62	1	C	-$62.00	$59.00
11/19/18	S C	11/30/18	$149.00	$0.10	1	C	$10.00	$69.00
11/19/18	B C	11/30/18	$124.00	$0.18	1	P	-$18.00	$51.00
11/19/18	S C	11/30/18	$120.00	$0.14	1	P	$10.00	$61.00
							Profit of:	$61.00

IYR – 11/5/18 – Broken Wing Iron Condor

After watching the market fall as a whole I felt there was good opportunity in a IYR Broken Wing Iron Condor with no upside risk. On 11/5 with IYR trading at $78.85 I sold the 12/21 $78 Call and purchased the $79 Call to cover. I then sold the $78 Put and Purchased the $74 Put to cover.

If I held to expiration my maximum profit could have been about $170.00 on a risk of $226.00. IYR Implied Volatility was 60.16 and the trade had a profitability probability of 66.18%. My estimated break even at expiration on this trade was at $76.26.

On 12/3 after 28 days my GTC order it and I made $48.00 on my risk of $226.00 or about 21.24% which was a very good return on this type of trade.

Date		EXP	Strike	Price	Ct	C/P	Cost	Balance
11/05/18	S O	12/21/18	$78.00	$2.36	1	C	$236.00	$236.00
11/05/18	B O	12/21/18	$79.00	$1.72	1	C	-$172.00	$64.00
11/05/18	S O	12/21/18	$78.00	$1.85	1	P	$185.00	$249.00
11/05/18	B O	12/21/18	$74.00	$0.75	1	P	-$79.00	$170.00
12/03/18	B C	12/21/18	$78.00	$3.76	1	C	-$376.00	-$206.00
12/03/18	S C	12/21/18	$79.00	$2.80	1	C	$280.00	$74.00
12/03/18	B C	12/21/18	$78.00	$0.24	1	P	-$24.00	$50.00
12/03/18	S C	12/21/18	$74.00	$0.02	1	P	-$2.00	$48.00
							Profit of:	$48.00

EMR – 11/9/18 – Iron Condor

On 11/9 with EMR trading at $68.31 I entered into an Iron Condor position by selling the 12/21 $72.50 Call and purchasing he $75.00 Call. I also sold the $65.00 Put and purchased the $60.00 Put to cover it.

I actually entered this trade as a hedge to an ongoing Diagonal I was struggling to make a profit on. This trade had more risk to the downside because of the $5.00 spread on the Puts as opposed to the $2.50 spread on the Calls. In retrospect I probably made a mistake there but the way the market had been springing up and down I decided to go with it.

When I entered the trade EMR implied volatility was at 50.48 and the trade had a probability of success of 55.51%. Of course, if I was threatened on the upside at least my Diagonal would be helping this trade out.

My GTC order was hit on 12/3 after 24 days for a profit of $42.00 on a risk of $395.00 or 10.63%. Not too bad for a hedge trade.

Date		EXP	Strike	Price	Ct	C/P	Cost	Balance
11/09/18	S O	12/21/18	$72.50	$0.55	1	C	$55.00	$55.00
11/09/18	B O	12/21/18	$75.00	$0.20	1	C	-$20.00	$35.00
11/09/18	S O	12/21/18	$65.00	$1.10	1	P	$110.00	$145.00
11/09/18	B O	12/21/18	$60.00	$0.40	1	P	-$44.00	$101.00
12/03/18	B C	12/21/18	$72.50	$0.05	1	C	-$5.00	$96.00
12/03/18	S C	12/21/18	$75.00	$0.14	1	C	$14.00	$110.00
12/03/18	B C	12/21/18	$65.00	$0.65	1	P	-$65.00	$45.00
12/03/18	S C	12/21/18	$60.00	$0.01	1	P	-$3.00	$42.00
							Profit of:	$42.00

SPX – 11/27/18 – Iron Condor

This is one of my monthly SPX Iron Condor trades and for the second month in a row I struggled with it. Normally about one or maybe two a year give me a problem, kind of rare to have two in a row but that is the way the market moves sometimes.

Because I had such difficulty with the last SPX Iron Condor I was expecting an easy time with this one on 11/27 when I placed the trade. With SPX at $2682.20 and Implied Volatility at 28 I sold the 1/18/19 $2870 Call and purchased the $2890 Call. I sold the $2400 Put and bought the $2380 Put. Both of my shorts were at around Delta 10 to 12 which was just what the strategy called for.

My initial credit was $602.00 on a risk of $3398.00, I set a GTC to keep about half of it. When I entered this trade it showed a 74.39% probability of success if held to expiration.

At one time this trade was showing a $200.00 profit but by 12/20 that had changed. With SPX down at 2470 my short Put Delta was at 32 so I started looking for an adjustment. I rolled my Puts down and out a week from 1/18 to 1/25 and down from 2400/2380 to 2360/2340 for about a $1.00 debit. I left my calls for the time being hoping for move back up so I could roll them down to get them on the same cycle.

On 12/27 SPX spiked up 100 points and I rolled my Calls to the 1/25 expiration and down from 2870/2890 to 2720/2740 for a $.65 credit.

This move reduced my potential profit but that did not really matter that much since my rules say if I have to adjust I change my GTC to about break even, which I did.

On 01/04/19 my GTC order hit and I closed this trade for a $28.00 profit or 0.82% over 38 days. Not much of a profit but no losses and I defended this trade successfully.

Date		EXP	Strike	Price	Ct	C/P	Cost	Balance
11/27/18	S O	01/18/19	$2,870.00	$6.05	2	C	$1,210.00	$1,210.00
11/27/18	B O	01/18/19	$2,890.00	$4.30	2	C	-$868.00	$342.00
11/27/18	S O	01/18/19	$2,400.00	$11.35	2	P	$2,270.00	$2,612.00

11/27/18	B O	01/18/19	$2,380.00	$10.05	2	P	-$2,010.00	$602.00
12/20/18	B C	01/18/19	$2,400.00	$37.25	2	P	-$7,452.00	-$6,850.00
12/20/18	S C	01/18/19	$2,380.00	$32.40	2	P	$6,480.00	-$370.00
12/20/18	S O	01/25/19	$2,360.00	$33.10	2	P	$6,620.00	$6,250.00
12/20/18	B O	01/25/19	$2,340.00	$29.25	2	P	-$5,852.00	$398.00
12/27/18	B C	01/18/19	$2,870.00	$0.30	2	C	-$60.00	$338.00
12/27/18	S C	01/18/19	$2,890.00	$0.15	2	C	$30.00	$368.00
12/27/18	S O	01/25/19	$2,720.00	$3.05	2	C	$610.00	$978.00
12/27/18	B O	01/25/19	$2,740.00	$2.25	2	C	-$458.00	$520.00
01/04/19	B C	01/25/19	$2,720.00	$0.55	2	C	-$110.00	$410.00
01/04/19	S C	01/25/19	$2,740.00	$0.40	2	C	$80.00	$490.00
01/04/19	B C	01/25/19	$2,360.00	$13.05	2	P	-$2,610.00	-$2,120.00
01/04/19	S C	01/25/19	$2,340.00	$10.75	2	P	$2,148.00	$28.00
							Profit of:	$28.00

CAT – 11/28/18 – Iron Condor

CAT has been good to me in the past trading different types of Condors so I always take a look at it to see if there is enough premium to trade.

On 11/28 I was able to get a good premium on an Iron Condor primarily because Implied Volatility was at 82.41 which was pretty high for CAT. I sold the 1/18/19 $145 Call and purchased the $150 Call. I sold the $115 Put and purchased the $110 Put. I was able to get a credit of $1.32 on a risk of $3.68 per contract. I set my GTC at about

$.70.

When I started the trade it showed about a 62.06% of profitability if I held to expiration.

CAT had been at a loss or small gain for the majority of the trade so on 12/31 when I saw I could close it for $.74 I decided to go ahead and take my profit and move on. I had some losses on these trades over the past few months so wanted to take advantage of a chance to get out at close to my goal before the market dropped again.

I closed the trade for a $50.00 profit on a risk of $368.00 or 13.59% after 33 days. A good return. CAT was at $126.86 when I closed the trade and Implied Volatility had dropped to 67.86.

Date		EXP	Strike	Price	Ct	C/P	Cost	Balance
11/28/18	S O	01/18/19	$145.00	$1.46	1	C	$146.00	$146.00
11/28/18	B O	01/18/19	$150.00	$0.81	1	C	-$81.00	$65.00
11/28/18	S O	01/18/19	$115.00	$1.87	1	P	$187.00	$252.00
11/28/18	B O	01/18/19	$110.00	$1.20	1	P	-$124.00	$128.00
12/31/18	B C	01/18/19	$145.00	$0.24	1	C	-$24.00	$104.00
12/31/18	S C	01/18/19	$150.00	$0.12	1	C	$12.00	$116.00
12/31/18	B C	01/18/19	$115.00	$1.28	1	P	-$132.00	-$16.00
12/31/18	S C	01/18/19	$110.00	$0.66	1	P	$66.00	$50.00
							Profit of:	$50.00

V – 11/29/18 – Iron Condor

Seems like I am always trading V. I found a decent premium on this Iron Condor even though Implied Volatility was only at 32.49. It actually went up to 54.82 by the time the trade closed which meant I had to hold on to this one longer to wait on time decay to make me money.

On 11/29 I sold the 1/18/19 $150 Call and purchased the $155 Call. I sold the $125 Put and purchased the $120 Put. I got a $1.08 credit (not great) on a risk of $3.92.

When I entered the trade V was trading at $139.51, during the course of the trade it dropped to $133.31 by the time my GTC order hit. This caused Implied Volatility to spike but at least it stayed above my short Put at $125. The initial probably of success for this trade was 69.25% which is why I was still able to close for a profit even though V dropped quite a bit. I also allowed more room to the downside because of recent market activity.

On 01/02/19 my GTC hit and I closed the trade for a $46.00 profit over 34 days. My risk was $392.00 so my return was 11.73%.

Date		EXP	Strike	Price	Ct	C/P	Cost	Balance
11/29/18	S O	01/18/19	$150.00	$1.13	1	C	$113.00	$113.00
11/29/18	B O	01/18/19	$155.00	$0.41	1	C	-$41.00	$72.00
11/29/18	S O	01/18/19	$125.00	$1.04	1	P	$104.00	$176.00
11/29/18	B O	01/18/19	$120.00	$0.68	1	P	-$72.00	104
01/02/19	B C	01/18/19	$150.00	$0.06	1	C	-$6.00	$98.00
01/02/19	S C	01/18/19	$155.00	$0.01	1	C	$1.00	$99.00
01/02/19	B C	01/18/19	$125.00	$0.90	1	P	-$90.00	$9.00
01/02/19	S C	01/18/19	$120.00	$0.41	1	P	$37.00	$46.00
							Profit of:	$46.00

GS – 12/04/18 – Iron Condor

We found a pretty good Iron Condor trade with GS trading at $184.94 an Implied Volatility of 83.84 and a trade probability of success of about 61%.

On 12/04 we sold the 1/18/19 $205 Call and purchased the $210 Call. We sold the $170 Put and purchased the $165 Put to cover. We brought in an initial credit of $1.40 and set our GTC at $.75.

We opened the day on 11/11/19 showing a $42.00 profit and promptly watched it disappear. By the end of the day it had moved back up to $32.00 with GS trading at $176.04. We decided to take the money and run! Expiration was the following week so probably a good decision.

After 38 days we ended up with a profit of $32.00 or 8.79%. Time to move on to the next trade.

Date		EXP	Strike	Price	Ct	C/P	Cost	Balance
12/04/18	S O	01/18/19	$205.00	$1.46	1	C	$146.00	$146.00
12/04/18	B O	01/18/19	$210.00	$0.88	1	C	-$88.00	$58.00
12/04/18	S O	01/18/19	$170.00	$2.69	1	P	$269.00	$327.00
12/04/18	B O	01/18/19	$165.00	$1.87	1	P	-$191.00	136
01/11/19	B C	01/18/19	$205.00	$0.07	1	C	-$7.00	$129.00
01/11/19	S C	01/18/19	$210.00	$0.02	1	C	$2.00	$131.00
01/11/19	B C	01/18/19	$170.00	$1.83	1	P	-$187.00	-$56.00
01/11/19	S C	01/18/19	$165.00	$0.88	1	P	$88.00	$32.00
							Profit of:	$32.00

XLE – 12/11/18 – Broken Wind Iron Condor

I was able to find decent premium in XLE on 12/11. With XLE trading at $63.37 I decided to take a Broken Wind Iron Condor with no upside risk. My thought was the market was more likely to rebound from here. The advantage of these types of trades is that even if you turn out to be wrong you still might not lose money as opposed to a debit spread.

On 12/11 I sold the 1/18/19 $64 Call and purchased the $65 Call. I sold the $61 Put and bought the $56 Put. I had a pretty good range for profit and still got a good premium on this trade.

When I entered the trade XLE had an Implied Volatility of 84.25 and the trade had a 71.81% chance of profitability. I set my GTC order at $.83 which would leave me a small profit if it hit.

By 1/7/19 I was pretty frustrated with this trade. XLE was trading at 60.87 which was actually below my short Put. This trade had been at a loss for a while, so when I saw I could get out close to break even I decided to take advantage of it and close the trade.

I made a profit of $6.00 on a risk of $357.00 or 1.68% after 27 days. Not very good but I was just glad to get out of it.

Date		EXP	Strike	Price	Ct	C/P	Cost	Balance
12/11/18	S O	01/18/19	$64.00	$1.75	1	C	$175.00	$175.00
12/11/18	B O	01/18/19	$65.00	$1.33	1	C	-$133.00	$42.00
12/11/18	S O	01/18/19	$61.00	$1.55	1	P	$155.00	$197.00
12/11/18	B O	01/18/19	$56.00	$0.50	1	P	-$54.00	143
01/07/19	B C	01/18/19	$64.00	$0.24	1	C	-$24.00	$119.00
01/07/19	S C	01/18/19	$65.00	$0.12	1	C	$12.00	$131.00
01/07/19	B C	01/18/19	$61.00	$1.36	1	P	-$136.00	-$5.00
01/07/19	S C	01/18/19	$56.00	$0.15	1	P	$11.00	$6.00

KRE – 12/12/18 – Broken Wing Iron Condor

The market had gotten a little more volatile than I preferred for my range bound strategies. Yes, we need volatility to make money selling options but even to much of a good thing can be bad.

On 12/12 with KRE trading at $51.15 we decided to enter a broken wing iron condor in KRE with no up side risk. We felt it was about time for the market to rebound at least some.

We sold the 1/18/19 $53 Call and purchased the $54 Call. We sold the $49 Put and purchased the $44 Put for $1.06 credit. Volatility was at 69.14 when we entered the trade.

We set a GTC order for $.52.

On 1/10/19 we decided to go ahead and close the trade for $.57 instead of waiting for our GTC order to hit. Truthfully we just wanted to lock in some profit, probably could have waited but the market had been a little rough on us lately.

After 29 days we closed for a profit of $45.00 or 11.42%.

Date		EXP	Strike	Price	Ct	C/P	Cost	Balance
12/12/18	S O	01/18/19	$53.00	$0.90	1	C	$90.00	$90.00
12/12/18	B O	01/18/19	$54.00	$0.61	1	C	-$62.00	$28.00
12/12/18	S O	01/18/19	$49.00	$1.04	1	P	$104.00	$132.00
12/12/18	B O	01/18/19	$44.00	$0.25	1	P	-$26.00	106
01/10/19	B C	01/18/19	$53.00	$0.06	1	C	-$6.00	$100.00
01/10/19	S C	01/18/19	$54.00	$0.02	1	C	$2.00	$102.00

01/10/19	B C	01/18/19	$49.00	$0.58	1	P	-$58.00	$44.00
01/10/19	S C	01/18/19	$44.00	$0.05	1	P	$1.00	$45.00
							Profit of:	$45.00

Chapter 2

Spreads

There are a couple of different types of spreads I trade. Credit spreads which I receive money to place and debit spreads in which I pay money to place. Either can use either calls or puts.

With a credit spread we are hoping that the price of the security stays above or below our short position. With a debit spread we are wanting our long position to increase in value. I trade both although there are many experts out there that would tell you that you should never buy an option. I do not agree with that, I think there is a time and place for both.

There are some more complicated spreads you can trade but there is a lot to be said for keeping it simple. Many of the more complicated strategies I am convinced were designed by brokers just trying to increase their commissions. Yes, I do trade those from time to time. I have one strategy in particular that I trade that is a combination of a couple of different strategies that I will not introduce here. Might save that for an advanced options trading course.

HD – 7/11/18 – Debit Call Spread

I took this trade based on a bull flag breakout on the daily chart. There was a lot of daily support, strong price support and a continuing trend which made me think this was a high probability set up.

With HD trading at $196.33, I bought the $195/$200 call spread for $2.45 using the 9/21/18 expiration contracts. I set a mental stop at $191.76 and a potential target at $200.47 with 73 days on the spread.

On 7/13 I did not really like the daily candle and noticed some weekly resistance I had missed during my initial decision to take the spread. I decided to close for a quick profit when HD hit $199.43 and then bounced down off of weekly support.

Overall I ended up with a profit of $235.00 on a risk of $1225.00 or a 19% return in 2 days. Which is why I went ahead and closed. I still had confidence in the set up, but could not pass up the quick return.

Date		EXP	Strike	Price	Ct	C/P	Cost	Balance
07/11/18	B O	09/21/18	195	6.98	5	C	-$3,490.00	-$3,490.00
07/11/18	S O	09/21/18	200	4.53	5	C	$2,265.00	-$1,225.00
07/13/18	S C	09/21/18	195	8.4	5	C	$4,200.00	$2,975.00
07/13/18	B C	09/21/18	200	5.48	5	C	-$2,740.00	$235.00
							Profit of:	$235.00

SPX – 7/31/18 – Bull Put Credit Spread

This was supposed to be an Iron Condor but I could not get a fill I liked on the Calls side so I ended up with a Put Credit Spread. This happens sometimes but that is OK. I don't want to take a position I am not comfortable with just to get into a trade.

With SPX trading at 2816 I sold the $2620 Put and bought the 2595 Put to cover it for a credit of $1.25 on a $25 spread. As stated above, I was not able to get the Call side filed. After a couple of days of trying, I just left it as a Put Credit Spread.

On 8/27 my GTC order was hit to close the trade out early for a little over half what I initially got as my Credit.

After 27 days I ended up with a profit of $500.00 on a risk of $11,875.00 or about 4.2%. Annualized that is over 56%.

Date		EXP	Strike	Price	Ct	C/P	Cost	Balance
07/31/18	S O	09/21/18	2620	10.4	5	P	$5,200.00	$5,200.00
07/31/18	B O	09/21/18	2595	9.15	5	P	-$4,575.00	$625.00
08/27/18	B C	09/21/18	2620	2.1	5	P	-$1,050.00	-$425.00
08/27/18	S C	09/21/18	2595	1.85	5	P	$925.00	$500.00
							Profit of	$500.00

FB – 8/2/18 – Bull Put Credit Spread

FB had moved down quite a bit and I figured it was oversold based on the price action and technical indicators. I decided to place a Bull Put Credit Spread to take advantage of my analysis.

On 8/2 with FB trading at $175.33 I sold the $160 Put and bought the $155 Put expiring on 9/21 for a credit of $.60 per contract.

I set my GTC order to keep just a little over half the premium and waited. On 8/6, just 4 days later with FB trading at $183.81 my GTC order was hit and I closed the position.

I closed with a profit of $185.00 on a risk of $2,200.00 or about 8.5%. Not bad for 4 days work!

Date		EXP	Strike	Price	Ct	C/P	Cost	Balance
08/02/18	S O	09/21/18	160	1.51	5	P	$755.00	$755.00
08/02/18	B O	09/21/18	155	0.91	5	P	-$455.00	$300.00
08/06/18	B C	09/21/18	160	0.58	5	P	-$290.00	$10.00
08/06/18	S C	09/21/18	155	0.35	5	P	$175.00	$185.00
							Profit Of	$185.00

TSLA – 9/05/18 – Bull Put Credit Spread

TSLA had ALOT of volatility (even for TSLA) over the past week or so but I just could not see how it could go to much lower. With TSLA trading at $279.63 and a Implied Volatility Rank of 75 I was able to get into a very nice Put Credit Spread.

I sold the 10/18 $250.00 Put and purchased the $245.00 to cover it. The trade had about a 65% chance of profitability if I held to close but of course, I set a GTC order to get just a portion of the potential profit and take full advantage of price action and time decay.

On 9/14, after just 9 days, my GTC order was hit and I closed the trade with a $60.00 profit on a $380.00 risk. That was a 15.79% return over that time period. When I closed TSLA was trading at $289.90. At least short term, I called the bottom this time.

Date		EXP	Strike	Price	Ct	C/P	Cost	Balance
09/05/18	S O	10/18/18	$250.00	$11.65	1	C	$1,165.00	$1,165.00
09/05/18	B O	10/18/18	$245.00	$10.45	1	C	-$1,045.00	$120.00
09/14/18	B C	10/18/18	$250.00	$7.05	1	C	-$705.00	-$585.00
09/14/18	S C	10/18/18	$245.00	$6.45	1	C	$645.00	$60.00
							Profit Of	$60.00

Chapter 3

Calendars

Calendar's can be a good way to trade a range bound security.

I have a number of formulas I use to determine if a particular trade shows promise as a calendar. Most of them can be broken down into this simple statement. You want to sell more time than you are buying.

What does this mean?

When evaluating a calendar you need a short position that expires a number of weeks or months before your long position. I usually trade the next weeks expiring short and purchase a long 3 to 6 weeks after that. When I say you want to sell more time than you buy it means that you want the daily time value of the option you sell to be greater than the one you purchase.

Example: If next weeks option is trading for $1.00 and it expires in 7 days then the daily time value decay is $1.00/7 or $.14 per day. If the long option you purchase expires in 28 days and is trading for $2.00 then the time decay value of that option is $2.00/28 or $.07 per day. From a time decay stand point this option has potential as a calendar.

There is no 'correct' number of time decay difference I have found 'magical' I usually do not trade them unless the short is decaying 1.5 times as fast as the long and prefer if it is decaying over 3 times as fast.

The other thing you need is a range bound stock or one you are reasonably sure is not going to jump either up or down very much on you. I try to stay away from overly volatile stocks and never trade calendars around earnings or other news releases. Also watch out for major market news such as interest rate changes.

ATVI – 07/06/18

ATVI looked like it was in a pretty good range with possible upside potential. I decided to try a calendar trade to take advantage of pretty good time decay between my short option price and my long option price which is very important in a calendar.

With ATVI trading at $77.08 I decided to purchase the $77 Call expiring on 8/10/18. I shorted the $77 Call expiring in 7 days on 7/13/18.

Well, things did not go very well for me right from the start. On 7/9 ATVI was downgraded and the price action looked really bad. I decided to go ahead and close the trade for a loss. In retrospect, I should have trusted my initial analysis. Had I held this trade it would have actually ended up profitable. But...I didn't.

I ended up with a $128.00 loss on a risk of $434.00. That is a 29.49% overall loss. Yes, I still scare myself out of trades sometimes.

Date		EXP	Strike	Price	Ct	C/P	Cost	Balance
07/06/18	B O	08/10/18	$77.00	3.28	2	C	-$656.00	-$656.00
07/06/18	S O	07/13/18	$77.00	1.11	2	C	$222.00	-$434.00
07/06/18	S C	08/10/18	$77.00	2.14	2	C	$430.00	-$4.00
07/06/18	B C	07/13/18	$77.00	0.63	2	C	-$124.00	-$128.00
							Loss	-$128.00

RIG – 8/31/2018

I actually placed this Calendar as a hedge against a Diagonal trade I had going that had gone bad. RIG was not really a great candidate for a Calendar by itself, but I wanted to try and make something if it leveled out.

I knew I would not make any gain on the Diagonal if that happened so my solution was this trade. In truth there were better options but I had a Calendar on my mind so I let my tunnel vision put me in this trade.

On 8/31 RIG was trading at $12 so I bought the 10/5 $12 Put and sold the 9/7 $12 Put against it. My time decay indicator was at 196% which is really good but … things went bad pretty fast.

On 9/7 RIG had dropped to $10.80 and I was sitting at a pretty good unrealized loss on the trade. I really felt (hoped) RIG would go back up so I decided to roll the 9/7 $12 Put to a 9/14 Put. The problem is because of commissions I had to roll at a slight debit which is never good.

On 9/12 RIG had moved back up to $11.50 and I could have closed this trade for a $80.00 loss. I decided to hold another day. On 9/13 it had moved up to $11.67 and my gut was telling me it was time to get out before RIG took another nose dive. Just take my loss and move on.

My risk on this trade was $198.19 at its highest after the roll. I ended up with a $74.78 loss which was about 37.7% of my risk.

Date		EXP	Strike	Price	Ct	C/P	Cost	Balance
08/31/18	B O	10/05/18	$12.00	0.56	5	P	-$283.32	-$283.32
08/31/18	S O	09/07/18	$12.00	0.22	5	P	$101.73	-$181.59
09/07/18	B C	09/07/18	$12.00	1.21	5	P	-$613.27	-$794.86
09/07/18	S O	09/14/18	$12.00	1.2	5	P	$596.67	$198.19
09/14/18	S C	10/05/18	$12.00	0.65	5	P	$321.68	$123.49
09/14/18	B	09/14/18	$12.00	0.38	5	P	-$198.27	-$74.78

	C							
							Loss of	-$74.78

L – 9/5/2018

On 9/5 I noticed that L had been in a fairly tight channel for the past 30 days. One of the ways I look for a Calendar trade.

With L trading at $50.47 I decided to buy the 10/19 $50 Call and sell the 9/21 $50 Call against it. L was in the channel with a slight up trend and my Time Decay indicator was at 183%. On this one I entered a GTC order to keep about 50% of the potential profit for an early close.

On 9/11 I was up pretty good and decided to manually close early for a good return.

I was able to get a $100.00 profit on a $225.00 risk or about 44.4% over about 6 days.

Date		EXP	Strike	Price	Ct	C/P	Cost	Balance
09/05/18	B O	10/19/18	$50.00	1.35	5	C	-$675.00	-$675.00
09/05/18	S O	09/21/18	$50.00	0.9	5	C	$450.00	-$225.00
09/11/18	S C	10/19/18	$50.00	1.1	5	C	$550.00	$325.00
09/11/18	B C	09/21/18	$50.00	0.45	5	C	-$225.00	$100.00
							Profit of	$100.00

MCD – 9/5/2018

On 9/5 I was looking for another stock with Calendar potential and I found MCD trading in a pretty tight range. The Time Decay on this one was a little worrying at 108%. Which meant a large move could make this one difficult to adjust and still be profitable but I went with it anyway.

With MCD trading at $162.50 I bought the 10/19 $165 Call and sold the 9/21 $165 call against it because I felt there was a slight upward move in the trend. Because of the strike I chose you could argue this was more of a directional trade as opposed to a neutral one. I set a GTC order to keep about 50% of the potential profit for an early close.

On 9/12 MCD had moved up to $165.18 and I was sitting at an $80.00 profit. I decided to manually close and take the profits. MCD moving up toward my Strike really helped.

I closed with an $80.00 profit on a risk of $288.00 or 27.8% in just 7 days.

Date		EXP	Strike	Price	Ct	C/P	Cost	Balance
09/05/18	S O	09/21/18	$165.00	0.94	2	C	$188.00	$188.00
09/05/18	B O	10/19/18	$165.00	2.38	2	C	-$476.00	-$288.00
09/12/18	S C	10/19/18	$165.00	3.4	2	C	$680.00	$392.00
09/12/18	B C	09/21/18	$165.00	1.56	2	C	-$312.00	$80.00
							Profit of	$80.00

UNG – 9/05/2018

UNG was showing an Implied Volatility rank of 7.07 which suggested it would not move too much during the course of the trade. When we entered the trade we were showing a Time Decay value of 163%. We set our initial GTC order to keep about half risk amount as profit.

On 9/5 with UNG trading at $22.91 we bought the 10/19 $23.00 Put and sold the 9/21 $23.00 Put against.

On 9/21 UNG was trading at $24.61 and out of the initial channel we had identified for our trade. We were showing a $94.00 loss if we closed so we started looking for a roll. We ended up rolling this from a Calendar to a debit spread because there was no value in the $23 or $23.50 Puts. We ended up with with a $23.00/$24.00 debit spread. So, now we needed UNG to stay above $24.00 since this raised our risk.

On 9/28 UNG was trading at $24.69 and we were able to roll our $24.00 Put to $23.50 which reduced our risk and gave us a $23.00/$23.50 debit spread. We changed our GTC to break even just trying to get out of this trade.

UNG did not cooperate as it had spiked up to $26.05 on 10/5 well out of our identified channel. We had to roll our $23.50 Put to $25.00 giving us a debit spread of $23.00/$25.00 now and giving us the risk we used for this trade of $750.00.

On 10/12 UNG was trading at $26.38 and we considered one last roll but since we could close this for a $45.00 loss. We decided to just close and move on to the next trade.

We ended up with a 6% loss after 37 days on this trade.

Date		EXP	Strike	Price	Ct	C/P	Cost	Balance
09/05/18	BO	10/19/18	$23.00	$0.79	5	P	-$395.00	-$395.00
09/05/18	SO	09/21/18	$23.00	$0.47	5	P	$235.00	-$160.00
09/21/18	BC	09/21/18	$23.00	$0.01	5	P	-$5.00	-$165.00
09/21/18	SO	09/28/18	$24.00	$0.13	5	P	$65.00	-$100.00
09/28/18	BC	09/28/18	$24.00	$0.01	5	P	-$5.00	-$105.00
09/28/18	SO	10/05/18	$23.50	$0.02	5	P	$10.00	-$95.00
10/05/18	BC	10/05/18	$23.50	$0.01	5	P	-$5.00	-$100.00
10/05/18	SO	10/12/18	$25.00	$0.11	5	P	$55.00	-$45.00
							Loss of	-$45.00

KO – 9/7/2018

On 9/7 with KO trading at $45.65 I found another stock in a fairly tight channel. My Time Decay indicator was at 253% on this one which made it an easy choice for me.

I bought the $45.50 Call expiring on 10/12 and sold the $45.50 Call expiring on 9/14. I immediately set a GTC order to keep about 50% of the profit potential.

KO moved higher against me on this trade and threatened to break out of the channel I had identified. Perhaps I got lucky or perhaps my analysis was correct. KO spiked back down to $45.83 on 9/13 and my GTC was hit closing this trade out.

This one closed a $150.00 profit in just 6 days on a risk of $310.00 or about 48.4%.

Date		EXP	Strike	Price	Ct	C/P	Cost	Balance
09/07/18	B O	10/12/18	$45.50	0.63	10	C	-$630.00	-$630.00
09/07/18	S O	09/14/18	$45.50	0.32	10	C	$320.00	-$310.00
09/13/18	S C	10/12/48	$45.50	0.93	10	C	$930.00	$620.00
09/13/18	B C	09/14/18	$45.50	0.47	10	C	-$470.00	$150.00
							Profit of	$150.00

XRT – 9/7/2018

XRT was trading at a really low Implied Volatility of about 11.2 which should mean it does not move too much and make it a potential for a range based strategy like a Calendar. My Time Decay indicator was at 196% so I felt pretty good about this one.

With XRT trading at $51.37 I bought the $51.50 Call expiring on 10/12 and sold the $51.50 Call expiring on 9/14.

On 9/14 XRT was trading at 51.68 and I was showing a pretty good profit so I closed this trade for a profit.

I ended up with a profit of $84.00 on a risk of $390.00 or about 21.5% over 7 days.

Date		EXP	Strike	Price	Ct	C/P	Cost	Balance
09/07/18	B O	10/12/18	$51.50	1.07	6	C	-$642.00	-$642.00
09/07/18	S O	09/14/18	$51.50	0.42	6	C	$252.00	-$390.00
09/14/18	S C	10/12/18	$51.50	1.02	6	C	$612.00	$222.00
09/14/18	B C	09/14/18	$51.50	0.23	6	C	-$138.00	$84.00
							Profit of	$84.00

AGN – 09/12/18

On 9/12 I found AGN using a channel scanner and decided to put on a short term Calendar trade. With AGN trading at $189.79 I bought the 10/19 $190 Calls and sold the 9/21 $190 Calls against them.

On 9/18 this trade was showing a $60.00 loss and I considered closing but I felt price action would correct inside the defined range I had identified. The next day the trade was up $40.00 and once again I considered closing, which was probably the right decision. However, I waited another day to let my short time premium decay and was rewarded.

On 9/20 I closed the trade early for a $82.00 profit. This trade gave me a 14.5% return in about 8 days. Not too bad.

Date		EXP	Strike	Price	Ct	C/P	Cost	Balance
09/12/18	B O	10/19/18	$190.00	$5.50	2	C	-$1,100.00	-$1,100.00
09/12/18	S O	09/21/18	$190.00	$2.67	2	C	$534.00	-$566.00

09/20/18	S C	10/19/18	$190.00	$4.20	2	C	$840.00	$274.00
09/20/18	B C	09/21/18	$190.00	$.96	2	C	-$192.00	$82.00
							Profit of	$82.00

RTN – 09/13/18

I identified RTN as a tight channel stock over the past 30 days so decided to place a Calendar on it. This was another short term calendar. With RTN trading at $200.90 I decided to buy the 10/12 $202.50 Calls and sell the 9/21 $202.50 Calls against them to complete my Calendar

I placed at GTC order for about half the potential profit but ended up closing manually myself on 9/20 for a good profit with rising Implied Volatility.

I ended up making $126.00 on this one. My risk on this trade was my debit of $338.00 therefore my overall return was 37.3% 7 days. I wish all my trades went this well! The rising Implied Volatility was a big help and RTN did its part since it was trading at $201.09 when I closed.

Date		EXP	Strike	Price	Ct	C/P	Cost	Balance
09/13/18	B O	10/12/18	$202.50	$2.98	2	C	-$596.00	-$596.00
09/13/18	S O	09/21/18	$202.50	$1.29	2	C	$258.00	-$338.00
09/20/18	S C	10/12/18	$202.50	$3.20	2	C	$640.00	$302.00
09/20/18	B C	09/21/18	$202.50	$.88	2	C	-$176.00	$126.00
							Profit of	$126.00

KO – 09/14/18

KO had a really low Implied Volatility of 7 when I entered this trade. This along with the chart pattern is why I decided to place a Calendar on it. With KO trading at $45.85 I built a short term Calendar by purchasing the 10/19 $46.00 Calls and selling the 9/21 $46 Calls against them.

On 9/19 I was showing a slight profit. By 9/21 KO was trading at $46.55 and the position was at a small loss. The smart thing would have been to just close for a small loss but I decided to trust the chart and believed KO would move back down.

I decided to roll my 9/21 $46 Calls to 9/28 $46 Calls. I was able to bring in some additional premium which also reduced my overall risk to about $240.00, down from my initial risk of $336.00.

I kept a close eye on KO since I had rolled the position. On 9/26 with KO trading at $45.77 I decided to close early for a small profit. Once again on this trade I probably made the wrong decision and should have waited until 9/28 to close. The price action was still doing what I thought it would, but you just never know when something weird will happen so I closed.

I made $40.00 on this trade in the end. My initial risk was $366.00, based on that I had a return of 11.9% for about 12 days.

Date		EXP	Strike	Price	Ct	C/P	Cost	Balance
09/14/18	B O	10/19/18	$46.00	$.61	8	C	-$488.00	-$480.00
09/14/18	S O	09/21/18	$46.00	$.19	8	C	$152.00	-$366.00
09/21/18	B C	09/21/18	$46.00	$.55	8	C	-$440.00	-$776.00
09/21/18	S O	09/28/18	$46.00	$.67	8	C	$536.00	-$240.00
09/26/18	S C	10/19/18	$46.00	$.47	8	C	$376.00	$136.00
09/26/18	B C	09/28/18	$46.00	$.12	8	C	-$96.00	$40.00
							Profit Of:	$40.00

Chapter 4

Covered Calls and Diagonal's

Covered calls and Diagonals are one of my corner stone strategies that I go into great detail in my book Trade4Profits – Shortcuts to Profitable Trading. If you have already read this book you understand why I sometimes use a standard covered call and why I sometimes use a Diagonal option strategy. I suggest you read Trade4Profits – Shortcuts to Profitable Trading to fully understand but in a nutshell a Diagonal allows you to control more positions for less money. There is additional risk which I detail in the other book.

ATVI – 7/6/18

This was another of a series of trades I did in ATVI as I tracked it through a number of different trades.

This time I actually purchased shares of ATVI and entered into a standard covered call.

With ATVI trading at $77.06 I bought 100 shares and sold a $77.00 call that expired the following week against it.

This trade had a number of early problems as I watched price action and MACD. I also was concerned about an upcoming resistance point that I had not paid enough attention to before I entered the trade. Yes, I still sometimes make mistakes. It happens when you get in to much of a hurry and have to many trades going on.

On 7/9 ATVI spiked down to $76.25 in early trading on a downgrade. Because this happened so fast into this trade I decided to go ahead and close instead of trying to ride out as I will sometimes do in a covered call trade. I trade these a little different. If I had held this trade I would have been fine as ATVI recovered before expiration but I closed.

Because I took quick action and the price protection I get when I enter a covered call I did not take that much of a loss.

I lost $48.00 on a risk of $7597.00 or .63%.

Date		EXP	Strike	Price	Ct	C/P	Cost	Balance
07/06/18	B u y	100 Shares		77.03			-$7,703.00	-$7,703.00
07/06/18	S O	07/13/18	$77.00	1.06	1	C	$106.00	$7,597.00
07/09/18	S E L L	100 Shares		76.04	1		$7,604.00	$7.00
07/09/18	B C	07/13/18	$77.00	0.55	1	C	-$55.00	-$48.00
							Loss of	-$48.00

CELG – 7/31/18 – Covered Call

This is a standard covered call I entered in CELG. You will notice on the chart below how the price changed over the 37 days I was in the trade and how I defended my short Calls. The only mistake I made was on 8/31 I was going to allow the position to be called away but decided to roll for one more week. That decision cost me as the price dropped and forced me to manually close the trade on 9/6.

I probably could have stayed in the trade because I still liked CELG but I was in the process of closing an old trading account I had in which I was trading this position and decided to just close it and move the money to the other account.

Well, this trade won't make you rich overnight but I did make $114.67 on my initial risk of $8,915.61 which is about 1.29% over 37 days. This is a 12.69% annualized return. When trading covered calls it is the annualized return that is important. It probably would have been twice as high if I had allowed it to be called away the week before.

Date		EXP	Strike	Price	Ct	C/P	Cost	Balance
07/31/18	B u y		100 Shares	90.07			-$9,011.95	-$9,011.95
07/31/18	S O	08/03/18	$90.00	0.97	1	C	$96.34	-$8,915.61
08/02/18	B C	08/03/18	$90.00	0.5	1	C	-$55.60	-$8,971.21
08/02/18	S O	08/10/18	$90.00	1.21	1	C	$120.35	-$8,850.86
08/10/18	B C	08/10/18	$90.00	1.51	1	C	-$156.60	-$9,007.46
08/10/18	S O	08/17/18	$90.50	1.76	1	C	$175.35	-$8,832.11
08/16/18	B C	08/17/18	$90.50	0.65	1	C	-$70.60	-$8,902.71
08/16/18	S O	08/31/18	$90.50	1.83	1	C	$182.35	-$8,720.36
08/31/18	B C	08/31/18	$90.50	3.33	1	C	-$338.60	-$9,058.96
08/31/18	S O	09/07/18	$92.00	2.28	1	C	$227.35	-$8,831.61
09/06/18	S E L L		100 Shares	89.61			$8,955.93	$124.32
09/06/18	B C	09/07/18	$92.00	0.09	1	C	-$9.65	$114.67
							Profit of:	$114.67

BAC – 8/2/18

I decided to enter a Diagonal on BAC on 8/2. I have had good luck trading this stock in the past, which is why I chose it. With BAC trading at $31.14 I bought the 1/18/18 $21 Call and sold the 8/10/18 $31 Call against it.

BAC usually stays in a pretty good and predictable range. My goal is to keep selling weekly Calls against my Long term $21 Call which is very close to a Delta of 1 which means I am basically just paying for the amount the option is in the money and not much intrinsic or time value.

The market had started moving down more than I like so I decided to close this trade on 9/7. I probably could have stayed in this particular stock because it stays fairly range bound, but I also wanted to move my funds to another account with a much better commission structure.

In addition, if you notice I was assigned the stock. A lot of the time I will go ahead and close the position if I am assigned. Not really a rule of mine, just a good place to close mentally. If you do get assigned don't worry to much. Wait until the morning volatility is over and then close your positions. Your long Call still covers your short stock.

I ended up with just a $77.66 profit on an initial risk of $1,970.56 which might not sound that great at first. But that is a 3.94% return over 35 days or 41% annualized. That is a pretty good return in my Diagonal portfolio. Had this been a Covered Call the return would have been much lower because of the initial investment of purchasing the Stock as opposed to a near Delta 1 long Call option.

Date		EXP	Strike	Price	Ct	C/P	Cost	Balance
08/02/18	B O	01/18/19	21	$10.20	2	C	-$2,046.28	-$2,046.28
08/02/18	S O	08/10/18	31	$0.41	2	C	$75.72	-$1,970.56
08/10/18	B C	08/10/18	31	$.17	2	C	-$40.28	-$2,010.84
08/10/18	S O	08/17/18	31	$.40	2	C	$78.67	-$1,932.17
08/17/18	B C	08/17/18	31	$.04	2	C	-$14.28	-$1,946.45
08/17/18	S O	08/24/18	31	$.21	2	C	$40.67	-$1,905.78
08/23/18	B C	08/24/18	31	$.04	2	C	-$14.28	-$1,920.06
08/23/18	S	08/31/18	31	$.19	2	C	$36.67	-$1,883.39

	O							
08/31/18	B C	08/31/18	31	$.02	2	C	-$10.28	-$1,893.67
08/31/18	S O	09/07/18	30.5	$.37	2	C	$72.67	-$1,821.00
09/07/18		Assign	30.5	$30.50	200		$6,094.97	$4,273.97
09/07/18	B u y			$30.87	200		-$6,252.96	-$1,978.98
09/07/18	S C	01/18/19	21	$10.29	2	C	$2,056.64	$77.66
							Profit of:	$77.66

RIG – 8/2/18 – Diagonal

RIG looked like a good candidate for a Diagonal on 8/2 while it was trading at $12.83 and if you only looked at what it closed at 48 days later when I closed the trade at $12.41 you probably would have thought I was right.

The problem was that when trading weekly diagonal options large percentage price movements that occur right at your weekly expiration dates can really screw these trades up. That is one of the risks of weekly Diagonal trading.

On 8/15/18 I even added another contract to the position while RIG was trading at it's low of $10.59. This helped a little but not enough. I purchased another $6.00 Call with the same 1/18/19 expiration as my initial long Calls.

During the course of this trade RIG ranged from $10.59 to $12.41, as usually always at the worst times for me. I even tried to hedge this trade with a $12.00 Calendar position which just added another $74.78 loss to my total trade. Normally I have better luck on my hedges.

In reality it was the jump in price from $10.67 to $12.07 between 8/17 and 8/31 that wiped this trade out for me. I had to spend money just to keep the trade going and it pretty much locked in my loss for me. Probably should have just closed then.

When my 9/7 short Calls expired there was just not a good roll for me that didn't just lock in losses. So, I waited a week hoping for a major up move. In the end after 48 days I closed the position because it was close to a Pivot high and I was concerned it would head back down.

I ended up with a loss of -$180.63 or 5.44% on this trade. You don't always win, this was one of my losses. Max risk was $3,322.54 over the course of the trade. Really this loss was not too bad considering the fluctuation in price I endured at the worst times.

Date		EXP	Strike	Price	Ct	C/P	Cost	Balance
08/02/18	B O	01/18/19	$6.00	$6.96	4	C	-$2,787.60	-$2,787.60
08/02/18	S O	08/10/18	$12.50	$.53	4	C	$204.40	-$2,583.20
08/10/18	B C	08/10/18	$12.50	$.02	4	C	-$15.60	-$2,598.80
08/10/18	S O	08/10/18	$12.50	$.18	4	C	$69.35	-$2,529.45
08/15/18	B O	01/18/19	$6.00	$4.75	1	C	-$480.60	-$3,010.05
08/17/18	B C	08/17/18	$12.50	$.01	4	C	-$11.60	-$3,021.65
08/17/18	S O	08/31/18	$11.00	$.25	5	C	$120.70	-$2,900.95
08/31/18	B C	08/31/18	$11.00	$1.05	5	C	-$533.27	-$3,434.22
08/31/18	S O	09/07/18	$12.00	$.23	5	C	$111.68	-$3,322.54
09/14/18	H	Hedge	Calendar				-$74.78	-$3,397.32
09/19/19	S C	01/18/19	$6.00	$6.45	5	C	$3,216.69	-$180.63
							Loss	-$180.63

SMH – 8/3/18 – Diagonal

I like the way SMH was trading so decided to enter a Diagonal. The premium I was collecting was not great so on 8/17 I decided to sell the weekly's two weeks out instead of one week. I do this from time to time if I can't get enough premium or if the trade has gone against me and I am playing catch up.

When I started this trade SMH was trading at $107.26 and it was at $106.08 47 days later when I closed. Of course, the beginning and ending prices are not as important as how the security moves during the trade. SMH traded from a low of $103.96 to a high of $108.70 on the days I rolled my weekly positions. From a dollar value stand point this seems like a lot but on a percentage basis it was manageable.

I closed the trade on 9/19 after 47 days for a profit of $141.26 or 4.42% which annualized out to 34.34%. My maximum risk on this trade was $3,194.20. The main reason I closed here was I was changing brokerage accounts.

Date		EXP	Strike	Price	Ct	C/P	Cost	Balance
08/03/18	B O	01/18/19	$75.00	$32.85	1	C	-$3,290.60	-$3,290.60
08/03/18	S O	08/10/18	$107.50	$1.02	1	C	$96.40	-$3,194.20
08/10/18	B C	08/10/18	$107.50	$0.03	1	C	-$8.60	-$3,202.80
08/10/18	S O	08/17/18	$107.50	$0.73	1	C	$72.35	-$3,130.45
08/17/18	B O	08/17/18	$107.00	$0.03	1	C	-$8.60	-$3,139.05
08/17/18	S O	08/31/18	$105.50	$0.98	1	C	$97.35	-$3,041.70
08/30/18	B C	08/31/18	$105.50	$3.19	1	C	-$324.60	-$3,366.30
08/30/18	S O	09/07/18	$106.50	$2.64	1	C	$263.35	-$3,102.95
09/07/18	B C	09/07/18	$106.50	$0.72	1	C	-$77.60	-$3,180.55
09/07/18	S O	09/14/18	$107.00	$1.39	1	C	$138.35	-$3,042.20
09/14/18	B	09/14/18	$107.00	$0.11	1	C	-$16.60	-$3,058.80

	C							
09/14/18	S O	09/21/18	$106.50	$1.32	1	C	$131.25	-$2,927.45
09/19/18	B C	09/21/18	$106.50	$0.54	1	C	-$59.60	-$2,987.05
09/19/18	S C	01/18/19	$75.00	$31.29	1	C	$3,128.31	141.26
							Profit of:	$141.26

CSX – 8/15/18 – Diagonal

CSX is one of those stocks I just like to trade. I try to wait for a good set up based on daily price action before I get in.

On 8/15 I decided to enter into a Diagonal position. With CSX trading at $73.37 I bought the $45 Call expiring on 1/18/19 and sold the $73.50 weekly Call against it expiring in 9 days on 8/24/18. Of course, I don't plan on getting my position called away when trading a Diagonal. If I wanted that I would trade a true Covered Call.

The trade went very well. I decided to close on 9/7 only because I was in the process of changing trading accounts.

I ended up with a $350.53 profit on an initial risk of $5,552.56 or about 6.3% over 23 days. Annualized this comes to just over a 100% return which is awesome in my Diagonal portfolio.

Date		EXP	Strike	Price	Ct	C/P	Cost	Balance
08/15/18	B O	01/18/19	45	$28.55	2	C	-$5,716.28	-$5,716.28
08/15/18	S O	08/24/18	73.5	$0.85	2	C	$163.72	-$5,552.56
08/23/18	B C	08/24/18	73.5	$0.79	2	C	-$164.28	-$5,716.84
08/23/18	S O	08/31/18	74	$0.78	2	C	$154.67	-$5,562.17
08/31/18	B C	08/31/18	74	$0.26	2	C	-$58.28	-$5,620.45

Date		EXP	Strike	Price	Ct	C/P	Cost	Balance
08/31/18	S O	09/07/18	74	$0.72	2	C	$142.67	-$5,477.78
09/07/18	B C	09/07/18	74	$0.41	2	C	-$88.28	-$5,566.06
09/07/18	S C	01/18/19	45	$29.59	2	C	$5,916.59	$350.53
							Profit of:	$350.53

V – 8/10/2018 – Diagonal

V is one of my favorite securities to trade so you may see it a lot if you follow me on Twitter or our website.

On 8/10 with V trading at 139.98 I decided to enter a Diagonal option position by purchasing the 1/18/19 $110.00 Call for $31.50 which was pretty close to a Delta 1 option. I sold the 8/17/18 $140.00 Call against it the same day.

Over the next 35 days I would roll my short positions out another week or two depending on price action as I managed this position. I ended up closing the trade on 9/14 mainly because I wanted to move the money to another trading account with better commissions.

I made $247.99 over 35 days or about 7.87% which annualized out to 82.11% on an initial risk of $3,149.71. I was pretty happy with this trade, things went just about perfect for a diagonal. When I closed the position V was trading at $147.60

Date		EXP	Strike	Price	Ct	C/P	Cost	Balance
08/10/18	B O	01/18/19	$110.00	$31.50	1	C	-$3,155.60	-$3,155.60
08/10/18	S O	08/17/18	$140.00	$1.07	1	C	$101.40	-$3,054.20
08/17/18	B C	08/17/18	$140.00	$1.27	1	C	-$132.60	-$3,186.80
08/17/18	S O	08/31/18	$141.00	$1.91	1	C	$190.35	-$2,996.45
08/31/18	B C	08/31/18	$141.00	$6.10	1	C	-$615.60	-$3,612.05

Date		EXP	Strike	Price	Ct	C/P	Cost	Balance
08/31/18	S O	09/14/18	$143.00	$4.63	1	C	$462.34	-$3,149.71
09/14/18	B C	09/14/18	$143.00	$4.61	1	C	-$466.60	-$3,616.31
09/14/18	S C	01/18/19	$110.00	$38.65	1	C	$3,864.30	$247.99
							Profit of:	$247.99

COP – 8/6/2018 – Diagonal

COP was trending well and I thought I could make some money using a Diagonal. Unfortunately, price action moved against me at just the perfect times and there was just not enough premium when I rolled to new positions. I probably could have nursed more profit out of this one but I was changing brokerage accounts and decided to go ahead and close.

I entered this trade on 8/6 and rolled my short positions weekly to new positions a week out. Might have been better off rolling over two weeks but I didn't take that approach. There was more premium there but really not as much as I wanted even two weeks out.

When I started this trade COP was trading at $71.90, when I closed it was at $71.94. I know that sounds perfect for a Diagonal. The problem was in between it fluctuated between $69.99 and $73.28, always at the worst times for my weekly expiration's.

In the end after 36 days I closed this one for a $68.02 profit on a risk of $4,942.56. This was only about 1.36% but annualized out to 13.95% which isn't totally awful.

Date		EXP	Strike	Price	Ct	C/P	Cost	Balance
08/06/18	B O	01/18/19	$47.00	$25.30	2	C	-$5,066.28	-$5,066.28
08/06/18	S O	08/10/18	$72.00	$0.65	2	C	$123.72	-$4,942.56
08/10/18	B C	08/17/18	$72.00	$0.09	2	C	-$24.28	-$4,966.84
08/10/18	S O	08/17/18	$72.00	$0.68	2	C	$134.67	-$4,832.17

08/17/18	B C	08/24/18	$72.00	$0.01	2	C	-$8.28	-$4,840.45
08/17/18	S O	08/24/18	$70.50	$0.71	2	C	$140.67	-$4,699.78
08/23/18	B C	08/31/18	$70.50	$1.16	2	C	-$238.28	-$4,938.06
08/23/18	S O	08/31/18	$71.00	$1.24	2	C	$246.67	-$4,691.39
08/30/18	B C	09/07/18	$71.00	$2.36	2	C	-$478.28	-$5,169.67
08/30/18	S O	09/07/18	$72.00	$1.73	2	C	$344.67	-$4,825.00
09/07/18	B C	09/14/18	$72.00	$0.01	2	C	-$4.00	-$4,829.00
09/07/18	S O	09/14/18	$71.00	$0.54	2	C	$106.70	-$4,722.30
09/11/18	B C	09/14/18	$71.00	$1.34	2	C	-$274.28	-$4,996.58
09/11/18	S C	09/14/18	$71.00	$25.33	2	C	$5,064.60	$68.02
							Profit of:	$68.02

CSX – 9/12/18 – Diagonal

CSX, a stock I like to trade, was trading in a range I liked and showing support. I decided to see if I could make a little money using the Diagonal strategy.

On 9/12 I purchased the 2/15/19 $35.00 Call and sold a weekly $74.00 9/21 call against it. With CSX trading at $74.23 I had pretty good downside protection.

Notice I went more than a week out with my first weekly Call sell. I liked the extra premium as opposed to the shorter term Option. Gave me more downside protection.

Over the course of my expiration's and rolling CSX traded between $73.81 and $74.95. When I give these prices they are not the total swing during the period, just the price when I rolled or closed.

After 21 days with CSX up I decided to close on 10/3 for a

$266.00 profit. I made about 3.46% which annualized as 60.11% over the course of the trade. My total risk was $7,692.00.

Another reason I decided to close was that CSX had earnings coming out the following week. I don't really like to hold over earnings.

Date		EXP	Strike	Price	Ct	C/P	Cost	Balance
09/12/18	B O	02/15/19	$35.00	$39.47	2	C	-$7,896.00	-$7,896.00
09/12/18	S O	09/21/18	$74.00	$1.03	2	C	$204.00	-$7,692.00
09/21/18	B C	09/21/18	$74.00	$0.09	2	C	-$20.00	-$7,712.00
09/21/18	S O	09/28/18	$74.00	$0.54	2	C	$106.00	-$7,606.00
09/28/18	B C	09/28/18	$74.00	$0.35	2	C	-$74.00	-$7,680.00
09/28/18	S O	10/05/18	$74.00	$0.85	2	C	$170.00	-$7,510.00
10/03/18	B C	10/05/18	$74.00	$1.20	2	C	-$242.00	-$7,752.00
10/03/18	S C	02/15/19	$35.00	$40.10	2	C	$8,018.00	$266.00
							Profit of:	$266.00

SCHW – 9/21/18 – Diagonal

I liked the pattern on SCHW so on 9/21 with Implied Volatility at about 25 I decided to jump into a Diagonal trade. This trade did not last too long, or go like I wanted. SCHW was trading at $51.84.

On 9/28 when I needed to roll SCHW had dropped to $49.99 and there was not really any good premium I liked the following week. I decided to just hold and hope for a move up.

On 10/4 SCHW gapped up to $50.80, with earnings in a couple of weeks I decided to take advantage of my good fortune and close.

I made $138.00 on a risk of $4,260.00 or about 3.24%. This

annualized to about 90.95%. Not a bad trade considering that SCHW moved against me almost from the beginning.

Date		EXP	Strike	Price	Ct	C/P	Cost	Balance
09/21/18	B O	01/18/19	$30.00	$22.10	2	C	-$4,422.00	-$4,422.00
09/21/18	S O	09/28/18	$51.50	$.82	2	C	$162.00	-$4,260.00
10/04/18	S C	01/18/19	$30.00	$22.00	2	C	$4,398.00	$138.00
							Profit of:	$138.00

Chapter 5

Delta Verticals

The truth is that we do not trade a lot of Delta Vertical trades. They are primarily a time decay strategy that last about seven days or so. We have done fairly well with them but they are highly dependent on being able to pick the right direction of a stock over a short time period.

When we do trade them we typically do not risk much and keep them a VERY small portion of our portfolio. We also really focus on securities that are strongly trending and look for a pull back.

We rarely recommend these trades to others even though we trade them sometimes. If you do trade them, have a firm idea of when you want to close the trade if it goes against you. They can move fast.

A sudden unexpected drop in the stock due to news, earnings or world events could result in a max loss. Watch out for those and keep your positions sized correctly based on your portfolio.

MCD – 6/28/18

On 6/28 I decided to do a Delta Vertical trade on MCD. I decided to do this trade just because I like to trade MCD. Not exactly a great way to pick a trade, but subconsciously I have found you tend to follow stocks you like more therefore you get a better feel for them even if you don't realize it is happening.

Of course, you have to be able to get the right premium if you are going to trade a Delta Vertical no matter what. So...I at least made sure the numbers worked.

On 6/28 with MCD trading at $156.92 I bought the $152.50

Call and sold the $155.00 Call. Both were set to expire on 7/6/18. I paid $2.10 for the $2.50 spread which meant my potential profit was about $.40 or 19%. Not too bad.

My mental stop was at $155 because I had really strong support at $155.00. I was willing to let this one drop a little below $155.00 if I had to. It never really threatened the $155 level and I closed it on 7/6 for $2.48 With MCD trading at $159.84.

I ended up with at $195.00 profit on a risk of $1,050.00. That was a return of 18.5% over 8 days.

Date		EXP	Strike	Price	Ct	C/P	Cost	Balance
06/08/18	B O	07/06/18	152.5	5.12	5	C	-$2,560.00	-$2,560.00
06/08/18	S O	07/06/18	155	3.02	5	C	$1,510.00	-$1,050.00
07/06/18	S C	07/06/18	152.5	7.35	5	C	$3,675.00	$2,625.00
07/06/18	B C	07/06/18	155	4.86	5	C	-$2,430.00	$195.00
							Profit of	$195.00

SPX – 6/29/18

On 6/29 I entered a Delta Vertical on SPX. I like trading this strategies on the indexes because they are cash settled. Which means you don't have to worry about closing the trades out. They are cash only. Much easier to trade these types of strategies if you can get the right fills and areas you have good support.

On 6/29 with SPX trading at $2,738.94 I bought the $2705 Call and sold the $2710 call spread for a debit of $4.05. This means my max profit would be $.95 per contract or 23%.

On 7/2 SPX had dropped down to $2,707.80 which was actually below my mental stop at $2710.00, however the overall position was not showing that bad of an overall loss yet, so I decided to hold a little longer.

On 7/3 The market had moved up to $2729 and it never threatened the position again. At close of trading on 7/6/18 SPX was at $2761 so I just let my Calls automatically assign. When the dust settled I had a profit of $190.00 on $810.00 risk or 23.5%.

Date		EXP	Strike	Price	Ct	C/P	Cost	Balance
06/29/18	B O	07/06/18	2705	41.7	2	C	-$8,340.00	-$8,340.00
06/29/18	S O	07/06/18	2710	37.65	2	C	$7,530.00	-$810.00
07/06/18	A S	07/06/18	2705	56	2	C	$11,200.00	$10,390.00
07/06/18	A S	07/06/18	2710	51	2	C	-$10,200.00	$190.00
							Profit of	$190.00

CHTR – 7/13/18

On 7/13 I saw a potential opportunity with CHTR. Looking at the Delta's on the ITM Calls I decided to purchase the $295 and sell the $300 calls with CHTR trading at 305.30. Both Calls were for the 7/20 expiration, or 7 days away.

I got into this trade for a debit spread of $3.55. At max profit this position would be worth about $5.00, so I could potentially profit $1.45 per contract or about $725.00 on a $1,175.00 risk.

I set a mental stop of if CHTR traded below $301 I would consider closing.

Unfortunately, on 7/18 it hit my mental stop and I had to close the trade for a loss. Good thing I did because on 7/19 CHTR dropped down to the $292.00 level.

I took a loss on this one, but it could have been much worse had I not traded my plan.

Date		EXP	Strike	Price	Ct	C/P	Cost	Balance

07/13/18	B O	07/20/18	295	11.6	5	C	-$5,800.00	-$5,800.00
07/13/18	S O	07/20/18	300	8.05	5	C	$4,025.00	-$1,775.00
07/17/18	S C	07/20/18	295	7.65	5	C	$3,825.00	$2,050.00
07/17/18	B C	07/20/18	300	4.2	5	C	-$2,100.00	-$50.00
							Loss of	-$50.00

SPX – 07/06/18

SPX had a massive up day and I decided to take a chance on a trade with the expectation that SPX would stay above a support area I had identified. Really a massive up day is not the best time to make this type of trade.

With SPX trading at $2761.51 I bought the $2735 Calls and sold the $2740 Calls with an expiration of 7/13/18 for a debit of $4.00. At expiration if everything went right the spread should be worth $5.00 giving me a profit of $1.00 or 25% based on the $4.00 risk.

On 7/10 SPX was trading at 2791 however I was not really liking the daily candle plus having second thoughts about my decision to enter this on a massive up day so I started trying to close with whatever profit I could.

I was able to close this one early for a profit of $170.00 on a risk of $780.00. Return was 21.8% for 4 days.

Date		EXP	Strike	Price	Ct	C/P	Cost	Balance
07/06/18	B O	07/13/18	2735	34.2	2	C	-$6,840.00	-$6,840.00
07/06/18	S O	07/13/18	2740	30.3	2	C	$6,060.00	-$780.00
07/10/18	S C	07/13/18	2735	53.1	2	C	$10,620.00	$9,840.00
07/10/18	B C	07/13/18	2740	48.35	2	C	-$9,670.00	$170.00

						Profit of:	$170.00

ATVI – 7/6/18

I actually did this trade because I was trading ATVI in a calendar and a covered call. I was just curious how the different trades would preform as they all experienced the same price movements.

With ATVI trading at $77.04 I bought the $75.00 Call and sold the $76.00 call with both expiring on 7/13. I was able to open this $1.00 spread for $.74 giving me a potential profit of $.26 per contract or 35%.

On 7/9/18 ATVI broke down hard on a downgrade and hit my mental stop. Had I held this trade it would have ended up profitable, but I followed my stop and closed it.

I ended up losing $60.00 on a risk of $370.00 or about 16%.

Date		EXP	Strike	Price	Ct	C/P	Cost	Balance
07/06/18	B O	07/13/18	$75.00	2.44	5	C	-$1,220.00	-$1,220.00
07/06/18	S O	07/13/18	$76.00	1.7	5	C	$850.00	-$370.00
07/09/18	S C	07/13/18	$75.00	1.53	5	C	$765.00	$395.00
07/09/18	B C	07/13/18	$76.00	0.91	5	C	-$455.00	-$60.00
							Loss of	-$60.00

AMZN – 7/9/18

I decided to enter this trade on a Monday instead of Friday like I had been doing. Wanted to reduce my exposure in the market when I could. Both SPX and AMZN are up pretty good today, so not the ideal time to enter this trade but I liked the options premium's and delta's I saw so took a chance.

With AMZN trading at 1729.04 I bought the $1702.50 Call and sold the $1705.00 Call both expiring on Friday 7/13/18. AMZN can have some pretty good swings so you really have to manage this one and try to time it so the first day or two go your way based on previous price action.

I was able to get into this spread for about $1.98 for the $2.50 spread. Theoretically I could profit as much as $.52 per contract on $1.98 risk or 26%.

Things went pretty well with AMZN trading at $1744 the day after I entered the trade. On 7/12, the day before expiration AMZN was trading at $1787 so I decided to go ahead and exit at close to max profit. Why wait another day, just in case. Plus, I typically have a number of trades to manage on Friday's so it is already helpful if I can get out of one early.

I was able to get a profit of $104.00 on a risk of $396.00 or about a 26% over 4 days.

Date		EXP	Strike	Price	Ct	C/P	Cost	Balance
07/09/18	B O	07/13/18	$1,702.50	32.73	2	C	-$6,546.00	-$6,546.00
07/09/18	S O	07/13/18	$1,705.00	30.75	2	C	$6,150.00	-$396.00
07/13/18	S C	07/13/18	$1,702.50	109.43	2	C	$21,866.00	$21,490.00
07/13/18	B C	07/13/18	$1,705.00	106.93	2	C	-$21,386.00	$104.00
							Profit of:	$104.00

GOOG – 07/09/18

Trading this one on a Monday also to avoid some of the weekend risk. I think I may like these types of trades better on Monday's as opposed to Friday entries.

With GOOG trading at 1146.33 I bought the $1130 Call and sold the $1132.50 Call both expiring on Friday 7/13/18 for a $1.95 debit on a $2.50 potential spread. I could make up to $.55 per contract or about 28% based my debit.

On 7/10 GOOG was trading at 1158.76 which was good. On 7/12 GOOG was at 1180 so I decided to go ahead and try to close early instead of risking another day and to give me less to do on Friday.

Closed for a profit of $110.00 on a risk of $390.00 or 28%.

Date		EXP	Strike	Price	Ct	C/P	Cost	Balance
07/09/18	B O	07/13/18	$1,130.00	20.75	2	C	-$4,150.00	-$4,150.00
07/09/18	S O	07/13/18	$1,132.50	18.8	2	C	$3,760.00	-$390.00
07/13/18	S C	07/13/18	$1,130.00	62.28	2	C	$12,456.00	$12,066.00
07/13/18	B C	07/13/18	$1,132.50	59.78	2	C	-$11,956.00	$110.00
							Profit:	$110.00

CHTR – 7/13/18

On 7/13 I decided to place a Delta Vertical position in CHTR while it was trading at 305.30. I felt I had a good entry point and a favorable spread.

I bought the $295 and sold the $300 Calls which were scheduled to expire 7 days later on 7/20 for a $3.55 debit on a $5.00 spread. If everything worked out I would have made $1.45 per spread or about 41%.

On 7/17 CHTR hit my mental stop and I started watching closely. On 7/18 I decided to close with CHTR trading at $302.03 which was just above my short call. Turns out, following my mental stopped saved me this time. CHTR broke down hard on 7/19 to the $292.00 level.

I finished with a loss of $25.00 on a risk of $1,750.00 or about 1.4%.

Date		EXP	Strike	Price	Ct	C/P	Cost	Balance
07/13/18	B O	07/20/18	$295.00	11.6	5	C	-$5,800.00	-$5,800.00
07/13/18	S O	07/20/18	$300.00	8.05	5	C	$4,050.00	-$1,750.00
07/18/18	S C	07/20/18	$295.00	7.65	5	C	$3,825.00	$2,075.00
07/18/18	B C	07/20/18	$300.00	4.2	5	C	-$2,100.00	-$25.00
							Loss of	-$25.00

BBY – 9/4/18

On 9/4 I thought I had found a good candidate for a Delta Vertical trade.

With BBY trading at $80.19 I bought the $78 Call and sold the $79 Call both expiring on 9/7. I bought the $1 spread for $.64 so I could have made $.36 per contract or about 56% which was really good.

I entered the trade first thing in the morning on 9/4 which was probably a mistake. Should have waited for morning volatility to die down. BBY went up then began to pull back with the overall market.

I had been in the trade for less than 20 minutes when my mental stop of $79 was hit. I liked the daily chart pattern so I decided to hold.

On 9/5 I was still watching but beginning to get concerned about the price action during the day. I finally decided to close since my mental stop was actually hit yesterday. BBY was trading at $78.93 when I closed.

Even though this hit my mental stop I still only lost $10.00 on the trade. My risk was $320.00 so I lost 3.13%. Not great but one of the things I like about the Delta Vertical trades is that you can get good returns with little risk (or loss) provided you aggressively follow your mental stops.

Of course, a sudden unexpected drop in the stock due to news, earnings or world events could result in a max loss. Watch out for those and keep your positions sized correctly based on your portfolio (as I stated in the description of these trades).

Date		EXP	Strike	Price	Ct	C/P	Cost	Balance
09/04/18	B O	09/07/18	$78.00	2.13	5	C	-$1,065.00	-$1,065.00
09/04/18	S O	09/07/18	$79.00	1.49	5	C	$745.00	-$320.00
09/05/18	S C	09/07/18	$78.00	1.46	5	C	$730.00	$410.00
09/05/18	B C	09/07/18	$79.00	0.84	5	C	-$420.00	-$10.00
							Loss of:	-$10.00

SPX – 9/10/18

On 9/10 SPX looked like a good candidate for a quick Delta Vertical trade. Looked like it was in a solid up move with good support.

With SPX trading at $2882.55 I Bought the 9/14 $2855.00 and sold the $2860.00 Calls.

On 9/11, after just one day my GTC order was hit and I brought in a profit of $280.00 on a risk of $780.00. That was a 35.90% return, this time it annualized as 13102.56%! Really the annualized return on these is not that important since there is no way you could trade them continuously. I just like to put it in there for shock and awe value.

I was actually able to close these at more than the spread because of a big volatility spike. This is also not a normal event. This trade is not continually repeatable but it does show what can happen when things get volatile. Of course, it can have the opposite effect also.

Date		EXP	Strike	Price	Ct	C/P	Cost	Balance
09/10/18	B O	09/14/18	$2,855.00	$30.40	2	C	-$6,080.00	-$6,080.00
09/10/18	S O	09/14/18	$2,860.00	$26.50	2	C	$5,300.00	-$780.00

09/11/18	S C	09/14/18	$2,855.00	$33.40	2	C	$6,680.00	$5,900.00
09/11/18	B C	09/14/18	$2,860.00	$28.10	2	C	-$5,620.00	$280.00
							Profit of:	$280.00

Chapter 6

Miscellaneous Trades

This section has a number of other trades I wanted to show you. Two of them are pretty simple, the long call and the long put. When you purchase a call you are expecting the underlying security to go up in price. It is much cheaper to purchase a call than the stock itself. If done correctly you can take almost full advantage of an up move in the stock with your risk limited to the price of the call. Watch out for time decay, which can make a slightly positive trade into a loss.

Long puts are essentially the opposite of a long call in that you expect the price of the underlying security to go down and you want to take advantage of that. As the price goes down, you make money. As with the long call watch out for time decay in a slightly positive trade because it can leave you with a loss. Your profit can be almost as good as if you shorted the stock with your risk limited to the price you paid for the put.

Strangles are another one I put in this section. Mainly just to introduce you to them.

I also show you butterfly option trades. This is just as an introduction to them. I have been using them more lately but they can be difficult to manage if you spend to much to get into one. Also, if you are using a trade calculator showing your maximum profit remember that is if you hold the position until expiration and it finishes at exactly the price of your short. That rarely happens. I usually close butterfly's early for a reasonable return. What is reasonable? Depends on what you paid to get into it. I try to limit my risk, so I shoot for a higher percentage return. However, that may only be half what the potential was.

Pay attention, there is a difference when you sell or buy a butterfly or strangle. When you sell them your probably of success if you set them up right should be MUCH greater, but your return will be a lot lower.

By comparison when you buy a strangle or butterfly you will usually spend less money (less risk) which means better returns but your probability of success is MUCH lower.

We typically sell butterflys and strangles as part of our overall trading strategy but every once in a while you will find us on the buyer side.

If enough of people are interested I will write some more about butterfly's on my website (www.trade4profits.com). I have found them to be very interesting. Yes you can make more money with a debit spread but you take less risk with a similarly structured butterfly. With that lower risk your returns are not as good, but you did get lower risk.

RHT – 7/11/18 – Long Call

RHT had strong fundamentals and had recently gapped down on earnings, even though they met earnings. It was bouncing off weekly support so I decided to purchase Calls. I chose Calls that were only 39 days out so I needed a fast move before time decay started to take effect and forced me to close.

The way I saw the position, my mental stop was at $137.39 and my target was at about $147.73 with RHT currently trading at $142.25. Not a great risk versus reward trade.

On 7/12 RHT had moved up to $146.78 and I decided to close for a quick profit. Probably should have scaled out but with all my other positions I decided to take the profit and run. Plus, I really did not have enough time on these options. Another mistake I made.

Overall I ended up with a profit of $450.00 on a potential risk of $780.00 or about 57.7%

Date		EXP	Strike	Price	Ct	C/P	Cost	Balance
07/11/18	B O	08/17/18	$145.00	3.9	2	C	-$780.00	-$780.00

Date		EXP	Strike	Price	Ct	C/P	Cost	Balance
07/12/18	S O	08/17/18	$145.00	6.15	2	C	$1,230.00	$450.00
							Profit of:	$450.00

PCAR – 7/12/18 – Long Put

On 7/12 I noticed and evening start pattern on the PCAR chart and decided to trade it. I purchased an ITM Put option with a Delta of 71 so I would make money a little faster if the stock continued down. I had to pay a little more for it but that is the price you have to pay if you want faster option movement in relation to the stock price.

Unfortunately, the next day PCAR hit my mental stop and I decided to close the trade for a loss rather than hold to see if it proved correct.

I ended up with a $80.00 loss on a risk of $1,510.00 or about 5.3%.

Date		EXP	Strike	Price	Ct	C/P	Cost	Balance
07/12/18	B O	11/16/18	$67.50	7.55	2	P	-$1,510.00	-$1,510.00
07/13/18	S C	11/16/18	$67.50	7.15	2	P	$1,430.00	-$80.00
							Loss of	$80.00

CELG – 7/13/18 – Long Call

CELG had been in a sideways move after a down trend. I watched it move up then retrace just above weekly support and decided to purchase the $80.00 Calls expiring on 9/21/18 with CELG trading at $85.51.

My initial mental target was $87.58 with my stop around $83.47.

On 7/17 the 200 moving average was showing strong resistance. CELG had hit it and bounced back down 2 days straight. I could close this position for a small profit now but I decided to hold.

7/18 bounced off 200 day again, which was starting to worry me a little. Yes, it could be compressing before a huge up move or it could be getting ready to take a dive because of too many sellers at that level.

On 7/20 it bounced off the 200 moving average again. With earnings coming out next week and no desire to hold through those I started looking for the exit.

I ended up with a loss of $110.00 on a risk of $1,570.00 or about 7%. Turns out I should have held as CELG eventually did go up. I am not sorry I sold for a small loss, earnings are scary to hold through!

Date		EXP	Strike	Price	Ct	C/P	Cost	Balance
07/13/18	B O	09/21/18	$80.00	7.85	2	C	-$1,570.00	-$1,570.00
07/20/18	S O	09/21/18	$80.00	7.3	2	C	$1,460.00	-$110.00
							Loss of:	-$110.00

CTRP – 7/16/18 – Long Put

Looking at the technicals I decided to purchase puts on CTRP on a break down below a previous range below the 61% Fibonacci level and into a previous gap up area. Volume was not great so I was a little worried but decided to go ahead.

With CTRP trading at $44.27 I bought the $48 strike Puts that were expiring on 9/21.

On 7/19 CTRP had a massive down day to the $42.79 range and I closed half my position and moved my mental stop to just above a previous resistance level at $44.19.

I ended up holding the remain position until 7/30 when I went ahead and closed with CTRP trading at $41.96 and in a consolidation range. I had a good profit so, decided to take it and run.

I closed this position with a $300.00 profit on a risk of $880.00 or about a 34% return in just 14 days.

Date		EXP	Strike	Price	Ct	C/P	Cost	Balance
07/16/18	B O	09/21/18	$48.00	4.4	2	P	-$880.00	-$880.00
07/19/18	S C	09/21/18	$48.00	5.55	1	P	$555.00	-$325.00
07/30/18	S C	09/21/18	$48.00	6.25	1	P	$625.00	$300.00
							Profit of:	$300.00

WMT – 7/17/18 – Long Call

WMT was trading at $88.32 and I felt like it was about to break out based on the chart pattern. I bought the $82.50 Calls that expired on 9/21. I went with more ITM Calls because I wanted a higher Delta to move the option prices faster as the stock moved up.

My mental target for WMT was at least $89.27 with a stop around $87.34. Not a great risk/reward ratio but I only planned to take partial profit at $89.27 and let the rest go a little longer.

On 7/18 the WMT daily candle gave me some cause for concern. It almost hit my initial target of $89.27 but then pulled back hard. I probably should have exited but decided to stay in the trade.

On 7/20 my mental stop was hit and I exited the trade for a loss of $180.00 on my risk of $1,340.00. That was a 13.4% loss.

Date		EXP	Strike	Price	Ct	C/P	Cost	Balance
07/17/18	B O	09/21/18	$82.50	6.7	2	C	-$1,340.00	-$1,340.00
07/20/18	S C	09/21/18	$82.50	5.8	2	C	$1,160.00	-$180.00
							Loss of:	-$180.00

MU – 7/18/18 – Long Call

I found a chart pattern I liked along with some promising price action in MU on 7/18. With MU trading at $57.86 I bought the $52.50 Calls that were to expire on 9/21. Again, I bought the ITM calls because of the higher Delta must like the WMT trade above.

I completely missed this one. On 7/19 MU pulled back below my mental stop and I had to close the trade for a $230.00 loss on my risk of $1,470.00. That was about a 15.6% loss. I really have no words, I just missed this one. That is trading and it happens sometimes.

Date		EXP	Strike	Price	Ct	C/P	Cost	Balance
07/18/18	B O	09/21/18	$52.50	7.35	2	C	-$1,470.00	-$1,470.00
07/19/18	S C	09/21/18	$52.50	6.2	2	C	$1,240.00	-$230.00
							Loss of:	-$230.00

MU – 9/10/18 – Strangle

I used to trade MU a lot, just getting back into the swing of things with this security. I decided to take advantage of some sidways movement and good premium in the market.

This trade started out with about a 80% probability of success based on the strikes I chose and current movement in the security. I entered the trade selling the 10/26/18 $55.00 Call and the 10/26/18 $35.00 Put with MU trading at $45.04 for a total premium for $1.18.

I made a mistake when entering this trade, not realizing that MU had earnings on 9/20. Something you have to remember to check. So, I started watching for a quicker opportunity to exit than normal. Found the opportunity for a quick profit the next day.

Ended up with a $36.00 profit on a risk of $1,136.00 or about 3.17%. That doesn't sound great but I REALLY wanted out and if you annualized this it was about 1156.69%

Date		EXP	Strike	Price	Ct	C/P	Cost	Balance
09/10/18	S O	10/26/18	$55.00	$.76	2	C	$152.00	$152.00
09/10/18	S O	10/26/18	$35.00	$.42	2	P	$84.00	$236.00
09/11/18	B C	10/26/18	$55.00	$.51	2	C	-$102.00	$134.00
09/11/18	B C	10/26/18	$35.00	$.49	2	P	-$98.00	$36.00
							Profit of:	$36.00

BMY – 9/10/18 – Long Call

BMY was trading at a good point on the chart and I felt there was an opportunity for a quick profit based on price action.

On 9/10 I purchased the 10/19 $62.50 Calls expecting a move up in the near term. I set a mental stop and profit target, I actually missed my mental stop because the price action moved against me faster than I expected.

On 9/19 after blowing through my mental stop I manually closed the trade for a $102.00 loss on an initial risk of $182.00 or about 56.04%. Not a very good outcome, but sometimes price action does not do what you expect. BMY had actually been moving up but on 9/19 there was a large down candle, that is when I decided to bail figuring it would have downward continuation momentum based on that candle.

Date		EXP	Strike	Price	Ct	C/P	Cost	Balance
09/10/18	B O	10/19/18	$62.50	$.90	2	C	-$182.00	-$182.00
09/19/18	S C	10/19/18	$62.50	$.41	2	C	$80.00	-$102.00
							Loss of:	-$102.00

CRON – 9/11/18 – Long Call

I was closely watching the chart pattern and price action on CRON and thought I found a good trade opportunity. With CRON trading at $11.97 I decided to purchase the 9/21 $12.00 Calls. I set a mental stop for my loss and had a general idea of what kind of profit I was looking for.

Obviously, since I purchased a call that expired in 10 days I was expecting a fairly quick move and profit. By 9/18 with my time value decaying fast I realized that things weren't working out as I had hoped. I decided to close the position with CRON trading at $11.75 for a $84.00 loss on my risk of $174.00.

This was a loss of 48% in 7 days.

Date		EXP	Strike	Price	Ct	C/P	Cost	Balance
09/11/18	B O	09/21/18	$12.00	$.86	2	C	-$174.00	-$174.00
09/18/18	S C	09/21/18	$12.00	$.45	2	C	$90.00	-$84.00
							Loss of:	-$84.00

NKE – 9/12/18 – Butterfly

We sold this Butterfly on 9/12 with Implied Volatility at 72 and earnings scheduled for 9/25. Since we were short we wanted a big move away from our entry point.

With NKE trading at $82.44 we sold the 10/19 $77.50 Call, bought the $82.50 Call and sold the $87.50 Call. Our max loss would be $723.00 if NKE expired right at $82.50. Our max potential gain was $276.00

This trade DID NOT move like we wanted through earnings, at one point we were down over $250.00, but on 10/10 we got lucky and NKE had a major down day which triggered our GTC order. I say luck but we also had probability on our side, still you never know with the market.

We closed with a profit of $76.00 after 28 days or 10.51%.

Your return is lower when you sell a Butterfly as opposed to buying one but your probability of success is usually MUCH higher.

Date		EXP	Strike	Price	Ct	C/P	Cost	Balance
09/12/18	S O	10/19/18	$77.50	$6.15	2	C	$1,230.00	$1,230.00
09/12/18	B O	10/19/18	$82.50	$2.91	4	C	-$1,164.00	$66.00
09/12/18	S O	10/19/18	$87.50	$1.05	2	C	210	$276.00
10/08/18	B C	10/19/18	$77.50	$1.20	2	C	-$240.00	$36.00
10/08/18	S C	10/19/18	$82.50	$0.11	4	C	$44.00	$80.00
10/08/18	B C	10/19/18	$87.50	$0.02	2	C	-$4.00	$76.00
							Profit of:	$76.00

MS – 09/13/18 - Strangle

MS had been in a downward trend but was still moving in a somewhat predictable fashion, so I decided to place a Strangle on it.

MS was trading at $47.58 on 9/13 when I entered the position. I sold the 10/26/18 $50.00 Call and the $45.00 Put. The position was showing a probability of success of about 64% if held to expiration. The 52 week low as at $45.56 so I felt pretty good about my downside protection. I received a credit of $1.18 when I entered the trade and set a GTC at about $.90.

On 9/27/18 my GTC hit and I closed this position with a profit of $56.00 on a risk of $1450.00 or about 3.86%. Annualized at 100.69%. There was not much price movement as MS was trading at $47.77, however this sideways action caused the implied volatility to drop which enabled me to take advantage of time decay and a drop in implied volatility for a fairly quick profit.

Date		EXP	Strike	Price	Ct	C/P	Cost	Balance

09/13/18	S O	10/26/18	$50.00	$.61	2	C	$122.00	$122.00
09/13/18	S O	10/26/18	$45.00	$.57	2	P	$114.00	$236.00
09/27/18	B C	10/26/18	$50.00	$.52	2	C	-$104.00	$132.00
09/27/18	B C	10/26/18	$45.00	$.38	2	P	-$76.00	$56.00
							Profit of:	$56.00

INTC – 9/19/18 – Time Decay

This is a time decay strategy that I use from time to time. Sort of an inverse short term Diagonal trade where I am trying to take advantage of the effects of time decay on a security.

You usually need a high Implied Volatility to make these work and in truth I don't trade them a lot. Just putting a couple on here as an example.

The idea is you sell a near term option at a lower strike than your longer term option (a week or so latter). If the weekly expiration's are a week apart you need to get into these at a credit. That way you make money if the security stays the same or moves down. Ideally, you want your short position to expire at the money or slightly below for maximum profit. The closer the position moves toward your long option as the short option approaches expiration the worse for you.

On 9/19 with INTC trading at $46.05 I bought the 10/5 $48 Call and sold the 9/28 $47 Call. Implied Volatility was at 36 and looked to be moving down. Showing a 75% chance of success. Max potential profit is about $108.00 and my max risk is $372.00.

On 9/28 with INTC trading at $45.65 I closed the trade for a profit of $44.00 or about 11.83% over 9 days. Not bad considering the security moved down. That is why it is important to enter these at a credit.

Date	EXP	Strike	Price	Ct	C/P	Cost	Balance

Date		EXP	Strike	Price	Ct	C/P	Cost	Balance
09/19/18	B O	10/05/18	$48.00	S.22	4	C	-$88.00	-$88.00
09/19/18	S O	09/28/18	$47.00	S.29	4	C	$116.00	$28.00
09/28/18	S C	10/05/18	$48.00	S.05	4	C	$20.00	$48.00
09/28/18	B C	09/28/18	$47.00	S.01	4	C	-$4.00	$44.00
							Profit of:	$44.00

IBM – 9/19/18 – Time Decay

Wanted to give you another example of the same Time Decay strategy I used above. Again, I don't trade these a lot. There are better options.

On 9/19 with IBM trading at $149.43 I bought the 10/5 $155.00 Call and sold the 9/28 $152.50 Call against it.

My break even on this trade is about $152.99 with a probability of success of about 75% since I was able to enter for a credit. Implied Volatility was about 55 and moving sideways when I entered the traded.

On 9/27/18, with IBM trading at $151.50 I was able to close the trade for a $104.00 profit. That is about 10.79% on my initial risk of $964.00 over 8 days.

Date		EXP	Strike	Price	Ct	C/P	Cost	Balance
09/19/18	B O	10/05/18	$155.00	S.20	4	C	-$80.00	-$80.00
09/19/18	S O	09/28/18	$152.50	S.29	4	C	$116.00	$36.00
09/27/18	S C	10/05/18	$155.00	S.33	4	C	$132.00	$168.00
09/27/18	B C	09/28/18	$152.50	S.16	4	C	-$64.00	$104.00
							Profit of:	$104.00

DIS – 9/19/18 – Butterfly

We were playing with the ThinkorSwim spread hacker and found this Butterfly that we could sell. It had an initial probability of success 72.76% although we felt the Implied Volatility was a little on the low side.

On 9/19 DIS was trading at $110.00 so we sold the 10/26 $112.00 Call, bought the $117.00 Call and sold the $122.00 Call for a credit of $.85. Our max risk on this trade if it expired right at $117.00 was $414.31 with a potential profit of $85.00.

Let me start by saying we did something wrong here. Our long Call was at $117.00 instead of $110.00 which is what DIS was at when we entered the trade. If we had entered this trade like normal we would have made money. However we basically said we think DIS is going to stay the same or move down, instead of just move.

DIS proceeded to move right up to our max loss position and even through it. On 10/10 we were showing a $117.00 loss with DIS trading at $115.55.

On 10/19 with a week left until expiration DIS was trading at $118.51 and we were getting concerned about a max loss based on the chart and no reason to expect a move over $122.00 or below $112.00. Therefore we decided to close and take the loss we had right now.

We closed for a $166.00 loss over 30 days or -40.77%. If we had traded this like we normally trade a Butterfly we actually would have made money. Sometimes we still outsmart ourselves.

Date		EXP	Strike	Price	Ct	C/P	Cost	Balance
09/19/18	S O	10/26/18	$112.00	$1.45	1	C	$145.00	$145.00
09/19/18	B O	10/26/18	$117.00	$0.35	2	C	-$70.00	$75.00
09/19/18	S O	10/26/18	$122.00	$0.10	1	C	$10.00	$85.00
10/19/18	B C	10/26/18	$112.00	$4.40	1	C	-$440.00	-$355.00

10/19/18	S C	10/26/18	$117.00	$0.98	2	C	$196.00	-$159.00
10/19/18	B C	10/26/18	$122.00	$0.07	1	C	-$7.00	-$166.00
							Loss of:	-$166.00

XRT – 9/20/18 – Butterfly

I bought an XRT butterfly on 9/20 despite Implied Volatility being much higher than I would have preferred. This was one of those 'gut' feeling trades that I do from time to time. Of course, it being a high potential return with only about 8 days until expiration helped make it worth the risk for me.

With XRT trading at $51.59 I bought the 9/28 $50.50 Call, sold the $51.50 Call and bought the $52.00 Call. Notice my spread was not the same between my Calls, not a typical butterfly.

My max loss here was my debit of $147.00, max profit would be $152.00 if it expired right at $51.50 (my short Calls).

I set my GTC order a $.75 credit which hit on 9/28 keeping about half my potential profit. I finished with a profit of $78.00 over 8 days or 53.06%. XRT was trading at $51.53 when my GTC order was hit. I might have been able to make more if I had held but that is not the way I trade.

Date		EXP	Strike	Price	Ct	C/P	Cost	Balance
09/20/18	B O	09/28/18	$50.50	$1.21	3	C	-$363.00	-$363.00
09/20/18	S O	09/28/18	$51.50	$0.49	6	C	$294.00	-$69.00
09/20/18	B O	09/28/18	$52.00	$0.26	3	C	-$78.00	-$147.00
09/28/18	S C	09/28/18	$50.50	$1.05	3	C	$315.00	$168.00
09/28/18	B C	09/28/18	$51.50	$0.17	6	C	-$102.00	$66.00
09/28/18	S	09/28/18	$52.00	$0.04	3	C	$12.00	$78.00

	C								
								Profit of:	$78.00

AGN – 09/20/18 – Butterfly

AGN had a very low Implied Volatility as I analyzed this trade. It had been in a very tight channel over the past 30 days so it looked like a good opportunity to purchase a Butterfly with a short expiration.

With AGN trading at $190.37 I bought the 9/28 $187.50 Calls, sold the $190.00 Calls and bought the $192.50 Calls. My risk on this trade was only $96.00 with a potential profit of $375.00 if AGN was trading exactly at $190.00 on 9/28. I set my GTC order to try and make about $95.00 on this trade.

Break even at expiration was $188.00 and $192.00.

On 9/26 AGN was trading at $188.16 and my GTC order hit. This time I was glad to have a modest GTC order out there as the price was moving toward my break even point and Implied Volatility was actually spiking up. Time decay did the trick and I closed for a profit.

I made $104.00 over 6 days on a risk of $96.00 or 108.33%. This was a good trade, although I could have just as easily lost the $96.00. When you see great returns like these it means there is a large risk of failure, that is why you get the returns. We look at these very carefully.

Date		EXP	Strike	Price	Ct	C/P	Cost	Balance
09/20/18	B O	09/28/18	$187.50	$4.00	2	C	-$800.00	-$800.00
09/20/18	S O	09/28/18	$190.00	$2.38	4	C	$952.00	$152.00
09/20/18	B O	09/28/18	$192.50	$1.24	2	C	-$248.00	-$96.00
09/26/18	S C	09/28/18	$187.50	$2.01	2	C	$402.00	$306.00
09/26/18	B C	09/28/18	$190.00	$0.79	4	C	-$316.00	-$10.00

09/26/18	S C	09/28/18	$192.50	$0.57	2	C	$114.00	$104.00
							Profit of:	$104.00

MU – 9/21/18 – Butterfly

On 9/12 with MU trading at $42.06 we decided to short a Butterfly with earnings coming up on 9/20. MU's Implied Volatility was at 80 and we started with a max profit potential of $260.00 on a risk of $738.00.

We started out with a $1.30 credit and placed a $.70 GTC order at the same time. To be profitable at expiration we needed MU to trade below $36.32 or above $43.70. Our maximum loss would be at $39.80.

On 9/18 our trade was up $45.00 with MU already up to $45.75 with earnings coming out on 9/20.

On 9/20 MU was trading at $46.28 before the earnings announcement. We decided we had more risk to hold through earnings than to close for a profit of $50.00 right now. So, we closed and took the profit.

We closed this trade after 8 days for a profit of $50.00 or 6.78%

Date		EXP	Strike	Price	Ct	C/P	Cost	Balance
09/12/18	S O	10/26/18	$35.00	$7.50	2	C	$1,500.00	$1,500.00
09/12/18	B O	10/26/18	$40.00	$4.05	4	C	-$1,620.00	-$120.00
09/12/18	S O	10/26/18	$45.00	$1.90	2	C	$380.00	$260.00
09/20/18	B C	10/26/18	$35.00	$11.45	2	C	-$2,290.00	-$2,030.00
09/20/18	S C	10/26/18	$40.00	$7.05	4	C	$2,820.00	$790.00
09/20/18	B C	10/26/18	$45.00	$3.70	2	C	-$740.00	$50.00
							Profit of:	$50.00

MU – 10/9/18 – Butterfly

Our last trade in MU worked so we decided to try another one. Implied Volatility was fairly low which supported buying this trade and the risk was so low that it was almost a throw away trade, sometimes we do roll the dice.

Plus, it was a fairly short term trade which at least psychologically made us think the odds were better than they actually were. We felt that MU would gravitate toward the $42.50 level over the next week or so.

With MU trading at $42.18 we bought the 10/19 $41.00 Calls, sold the $42.50 Calls and bought the $44.00 Calls. Our max profit was about $241.00 if MU finished right at $42.50 with a total risk of $58.00. We set a GTC for about a $120.00 profit and waited to see.

On 10/16, three days before expiration MU had moved back to $42.52 but our profit was still not at the $120.00 level. We decided to try and work on a close for this one and just get as much as we could.

On 10/17 with MU at $42.74 we closed this trade for a $60.00 profit over 8 days for a 103.45% return. Not too bad.

Date		EXP	Strike	Price	Ct	C/P	Cost	Balance
10/09/18	B O	10/19/18	$41.00	$1.95	2	C	-$390.00	-$390.00
10/09/18	S O	10/19/18	$42.50	$1.09	4	C	$436.00	$46.00
10/09/18	B O	10/19/18	$44.00	$0.52	2	C	-$104.00	-$58.00
10/17/18	S C	10/19/18	$41.00	$1.78	2	C	$356.00	$298.00
10/17/18	B C	10/19/18	$42.50	$0.67	4	C	-$268.00	$30.00
10/17/18	S C	10/19/18	$44.00	$0.15	2	C	$30.00	$60.00
							Profit of:	$60.00

SMH – 10/19/18 – Strangle

On 10/19 SMH was trading at $95.37 and trading right at the 200 day moving average. I started looking at possible Strangle positions and was able to enter one that put by downside break even well below the 52 week low.

I sold the 11/23/18 $102.00 Call and the $90.00 Put for a credit of $2.34 with a probability of success at 64.4%. When I entered the trade the Implied Volatility was at 56.16. It actually went up by the time I exited to 72.35 but time decay and a move back toward my entry price enabled me to hit my GTC order.

On 11/1 the position automatically closed at $1.65 giving me a profit of $69.00 on a risk of $1,300.00 or about 5.31% which annualized at 149.02% over 13 days.

Date		EXP	Strike	Price	Ct	C/P	Cost	Balance
10/19/18	S O	11/23/18	$102.00	$1.07	1	C	$107.00	$107.00
10/19/18	S O	11/23/18	$90.00	$1.27	1	P	$127.00	$234.00
11/01/18	B C	11/23/18	$102.00	$.62	1	C	-$62.00	$172.00
11/01/18	B C	11/23/18	$90.00	$1.03	1	P	-$103.00	$69.00
							Profit of:	$69.00

DIS – 10/19/18 – Strangle

DIS is another one of my favorites for Strangles, I like how predictable it tends to trade. There was a little bit of added risk here because DIS had earnings on 11/8 and the expiration for this trade was 11/9. If I was not able to get out early this could be a problem. However, this time I was aware of the extra risk so I managed the trade accordingly.

On 10/19 with DIS trading at 118.61 and an implied volatility of 58.25 I sold the 11/9/18 $123.00 Call and the $114.00 Put for a total credit of $2.62. The trade was showing a 65.44% chance of success if held to expiration. I put in a GTC order for $1.99 hoping for a quick profit.

On 11/1 after 13 days my GTC order hit and I closed the position for a profit of $126.00 on a risk of $4,000.00 or 3.15%. Annualized this comes out to 88.44%

Date		EXP	Strike	Price	Ct	C/P	Cost	Balance
10/19/18	SO	11/09/18	$123.00	$.61	2	C	$122.00	$122.00
10/19/18	SO	11/09/18	$114.00	$2.01	2	P	$402.00	$524.00
11/01/18	BC	11/09/18	$123.00	$.23	2	C	-$46.00	$478.00
11/01/18	BC	11/09/18	$114.00	$1.76	2	P	-$352.00	$126.00
							Profit of:	$126.00

MSFT – 11/27/18 – Strangle

I like MSFT for Strangles because it moves in a predictable manner, most of the time anyway. Just as will all trades, watch out for earnings.

I entered this trade with MSFT trading at $106.12 and a implied volatility of 48.98. The probability of success if I held to expiration was about 69.34% when I entered, but of course I never plan on holding to expiration so my overall probability of success is somewhat higher.

I entered this trade on 11/27 by selling the 01/14/19 $117.00 Call and the $97.00 Put for a $1.51 credit. I set a GTC order at about $0.94 to close this trade for a profit.

On 12/11/18 my GTC order was hit and I closed this trade after 14 days. I received a profit of $53.00 on a risk of $1,362.00 or about 3.89%. Annualized it was 101.45%

Date		EXP	Strike	Price	Ct	C/P	Cost	Balance
11/27/18	S O	1/14/19	$117.00	S.55	1	C	$54.00	$54.00
11/27/18	S O	01/14/19	$97.00	S.96	1	P	$95.00	$149.00
12/11/18	B C	01/14/19	$117.00	S.58	1	C	-$59.00	$90.00
12/11/18	B C	01/14/19	$97.00	S.36	1	P	-$37.00	$53.00
							Profit of:	$53.00

MCD – 9/13/18 – Back Ratio (Back Spread)

I don't trade many Back Ratio trades because of the risk versus reward on the trades. There can be a substantial risk for your potential reward. You need to be as sure as possible that the trade will work out and be sure to watch out for earnings!

A Back Ratio trade can be done with either Puts or Calls depending on the way you expect/hope the security will move. Ideally when using a Back Ratio trade you want the security to finish at or just below your long position. Ideally you want to enter the trade at a credit so you make money as long as the security does not trade over/under (depending on Call or Puts) your long position. You can also make money if it trades slightly toward your short position but that is where you start to get nervous. The closer it gets to your short position the more your losses grow.

On 9/13 MCD was trading at $161.94 with an Implied Volatility of 14.49. I bought the $150.00 10/26 Put for a total debit of $140.00. I sold the $148.00 10/26 Puts against this position for a credit of $324.00 giving me a net credit of $184.00 when I entered the trade.

The initial effect on my buying power was $7,300.00 so I used this as my initial risk. I set a GTC order which was hit on 9/21 and I exited the trade early for a profit of $96.00.

My return was 1.32% over 8 days. Annualized to about 60.00%. This was a decent return for 8 days investment but I still don't really like Back Ratio trades because of the risk. I rarely trade them and consider them to be a high risk advanced strategy.

Date		EXP	Strike	Price	Ct	C/P	Cost	Balance
09/13/18	B O	10/26/18	$150.00	$.70	2	P	-$140.00	-$140.00
09/13/18	S O	10/26/18	$148.00	$.54	6	P	$324.00	$184.00
09/21/18	S C	10/26/18	$150.00	$.40	2	P	$80.00	$264.00
09/21/18	B C	10/26/18	$148.00	$.28	6	P	-$168.00	$96.00
							Profit:	$96.00

Chapter 7

Bonus Items

Straight from our Blog at trade4profits.com

If you like these types of articles please visit our website frequently at trade4profits.com and look for new blog entries.

<u>* Options Greeks</u>

Do you know what Option Greeks are?

Do not worry of you don't most people either do not know what they are or think they are too difficult to understand to even try.

Good news, they are not difficult at all. Further good news, the main one we use is Delta so you do not have to be an expert in all of them. We also use Theta but it is not as critical to our trade as far as it's value when we trade, although it is VERY critical to us making money through time decay.

The others we sometimes look at are Vega and Gamma but we really do not focus on them much.

Delta – This is the most important of the option greeks we look at. In simple terms it represents the amount an options moves per $1.00 move in the underlying security. So if an option as a delta of .20 (20) then every time the underlying security moves $1.00 then the option moves $.20.

If XYZ security moves from $27.00 to $28.00 and you hold a long call with a Delta of .20 priced at $1.50 then it would now be worth $1.70. Keep in mind that Delta's are not static, they change as the security price changes. The more in the money an option is the higher its Delta will become until it approaches 1 which means the option price would change exactly as the underlying security price changed.

Theta – Theta is a measurement of how much an option price

changes per day assuming the underlying security price stays the same. So a Theta of .70 would mean the option price is decaying at $0.70 per day. This number can change depending on the underlying security price action.

Gamma – Gamma is an estimate of how much Delta changes if a stock moves $1.00.

Vega – Vega measures how much an option price will change per 1% change in volatility. This can be an important number if you are trading based on expected moves in volatility. While we do trade expecting volatility to move in a certain direction we still do not really look at Vega that much.

No, we did not forget about Rho, we just do not use it.

Some traders use Delta, Theta, Gamma and Vega when trading option positions. We have found that Delta and Theta are the most important to our trading style.

The best way to learn how the option Greeks change as the underlying price changes on a security is to paper trade some positions and keep a spreadsheet on Greek changes as compared to the underlying price and the option price.

Many of our trades are based on Delta values and use it in some strategies to determine enter and adjustment prices. We tend to watch Theta to see if the position is moving toward profitability for us.

* What is the Best Kind of Covered Call Trade?

This is kind of a trick question because we believe the best type of Covered Call trade is not a Covered Call at all. We prefer to trade Diagonal Option positions instead of a traditional Covered Call.

Let's start with what is a Diagonal Call trade, just in case you do not know.

A Diagonal Option trade consists of buying a long term deep in the money (ITM) lower strike Call Option and selling a shorter term at the money or slightly out of the money Call for income generation.

In choosing your deep in the money covered call look for one at least over Delta .90 so it moves close to the same as the underlying security. You also need it to be at least 90 days out before expiration or more. Sometimes we go as far as 180 days out.

Your short option is up to you. We typically start out selling an at them money Call expiring 7 to 10 days out when we start the trade to give us good downside protection. Yes, that means we might have to pay to repurchase and roll it if it finishes in the money.

We keep rolling our short option out 7 to 14 days each time it gets close to or expires. We do this as long as the underlying security supports staying in the trade.

Why do we prefer a Diagonal to a regular Covered Call? Simple, return on investment.

If a stock is trading at $60.00 then to purchase 100 shares will cost you $6000.00. If you can sell an at the money $60.00 Call against it for $1.50 or $150.00 and assuming you don't roll then your return on expiration if the position is ITM would be 2.5% ($150/$6000).

If you use a Diagonal Option trade and purchase the $35.00 Call Option for $26.00 or $2600.00 and sell the same at the money $60.00 Call for $1.50 or $150.00 then your return would be 5.8% ($150/$2600).

As you can see you can get twice the return using a Diagonal instead of a regular Covered Call.

When is a standard Covered Call trade preferred?

We can only think of one instance. If you are collecting dividends as part of a Covered Call strategy then you would have to purchase actual shares of the security to collect dividends. If you use a Diagonal Call strategy then you will not collect any dividends. But, the return is so much better who cares about dividends.

So, next time you are looking for a good Covered Call trade … think Diagonal instead.

* How to Find the Right Stock to Swing Trade.

First of all, there are lots of different methods to finding a good stock to swing trade and from time to time we like to discuss various options.

One our favorites is using two simple moving averages to determine a trend and the Commodity Channel Index (CCI) to pick entry points.

Depending on whether you prefer using options in swing

trading or buying the stocks themselves you could use these two indicators to trade long or short in the market.

We trade options both directs but prefer to look for long entries if we are buying the actual stock because we want to focus on stocks in the $2.00 to $15.00 range since those give us the most shares for the money. There are other things to look at like overall volume in defining a strategy but today we are just talking about the indicators.

You could use a number of different moving averages, we prefer to identify a little bit longer term trend so we use the 20 day and 40 day moving averages on the daily chart.

If the 20 day is greater than the 40 day we look for a long entry or an option strategy taking advantage of a move up in price. We use the CCI index to find an entry point. If the CCI is less than (-100) in an uptrend we look for an entry based on candles and price action.

If the 20 day is less than the 40 day we look to short the stock or use an option strategy to take advantage of a move down. Again, we use the CCI index to identify an entry point. In a down trend if the CCI is greater than (100) then we for an entry point based on the next couple of candles and price action.

Many times by just looking at a chart with the MA's and CCI plotted you can see just how well a security is predictable using this strategy.

Just remember a securities price action can change at any time, especially if there is news or earnings. What out for those things, they can really mess a swing trade up even for the best of us.

* 52 Week High Trading Strategy

Are you looking for a new ideas about finding a trade? There are a number of different strategies revolving around stocks reaching a 52 week high.

Today we want to discuss one that is worth taking a look at. Keep in mind we are not saying this strategy will work every time or should be implemented without taking into account the security being traded and the overall market conditions. Other factors such as volume when the security is making its 52 week high should also be considered.

All that being said, we just wanted to introduce you to an idea of how to find a trade based on a 52 week high.

First of all, as the name implies the security should be making a new 52 week high before you look at entering the trade.

Once you find a security making its 52 week high, you need to wait for it to pull back off the high to increase your chances of a successful trade. Yes, you might miss a sudden momentum move to the upside but your chances of finding a successful trade are much better if you wait for a pull back. Wait for the stock pull back and relieve some of the momentum. It will also allow the security to find new buyers to help it move back up.

Finding the right spot to enter the trade can be a little bit of an art, I typically look at the candle sticks or the price breaking the trend line back up after the pull back. Fibonacci levels can also be used to determine the pull back before a move up.

Why does this trade make sense?

First of all there are typically underlying reasons a stock is making a new high, We don't care about those since we are technical traders. We only care that it is happening.

Second, once you break to new highs there is no resistance to the upside. There is no technical way to know how much it will go up. There is no obvious selling pressure downward.

Third, waiting for the pull back off the high increases your odds of success and takes advantage of the sellers who decided to profit take at the high. I would not be surprised if many of them are buying back after the pullback.

Fourth, once it breaks the 52 week high the second time (especially if it is an all time high) who knows how much it will go up. We would want to do some profit taking after it breaks through because you can bet others will be doing the same.

* MACD Divergence Strategy

MACD (Moving Average Convergence Divergence) is a very popular trading indicator. It is in essence a trend following indicator that shows the relationship between two moving averages. The most used settings are the 12 period exponential moving average (EMA) and the 26 period EMA. The MACD value is calculated by subtracting the 26 EMA from the 12 EMA.

You can use other values, however for the purposes of the

MACD divergence strategy we use these work pretty well.

The most obvious strategy using MACD is when the 12 EMA crosses the 26 EMA, however this is really just a moving average cross over strategy you could do from the chart. Moving average crossover strategies are also not good strategies by themselves unless you are lucky enough to catch the beginning of a major trend.

We prefer to use the MACD divergence strategy to help us find opportunities where the security is overbought or over sold. We have found over the years that MACD divergence is fairly accurate in predicting a rebound or pull back before you see it in the price action.

This is NOT to say it is a perfect signal. Eventually it is usually correct but there can be a consolidation period which normalizes the MACD and then the security continues to move in the original direction. You have to use the price action on the chart to determine entry and exit points after you see a potential MACD divergence forming. Watch out for consolidation and be sure to take your profits. This strategy is used to signal a pull back or rebound not a change in trend direction.

When we talk about MACD divergence we do not mean that the MACD is still going up and the stock price is going down. People do what for this type of divergence but that is not the type of MACD divergence we like to use as a potential trade entry indicator.

We look at two types of MACD divergence.

One is when the stock prices are making new highs and the MACD histogram is not showing new highs. The opposite would the stock prices are making new lows and the MACD histogram is not showing new lows.

The second type is just like the one above but we use the faster EMA (12 EMA if using default settings) instead of the histogram. Other than that it works the same. We use the EMA divergence more than the histogram MACD divergence.

Again, after we notice the MACD divergence we wait for an entry based on price action, trend lines or candle sticks. We also not afraid to take profits and move our stops down.

Conclusion/Take Away/Risk Warning

Trading is a risky business and there is risk of losing money. Trades and strategies that work today do not always work tomorrow. Market conditions change.

We have done our best to accurately present our trades here but there is always the possibility of errors. Do not think that just because one strategy or another is profitable for us that it will be profitable for you.

There are many factors that may not be represented here that go into our into our choosing one trade over another on any give day. We also did not include all of our trades, we tried to include a good variety of them that represented how we traded during the time period this book covers.

Looking at our past couple of years we were curious how successful we were in our trading. Keep in mind that none of these success rates are guaranteed to continue tomorrow, these are just a look into the past.

In 2016 our overall success rate was 65.52%

In 2017 our overall success rate was 66.67%

In 2018 our overall success rate was 71.11%

In 2019 we are focusing a lot more on the high probability range bound strategies so would expect our success rate to move up even more.

We track our success by some trade types and wanted to share them here as well. We do not have these broken down by year, some of the trades go back a number of years.

In Covered Calls and Diagonals over the years we are 81.63% successful.

In Index (SPX, RUT, NDX) based Iron Condors we are trading at 82.50%

In Index (SPX, RUT, QQQ) based Credit Spreads we are actually at 100%. This is an anomaly and there are not a lot of trades because we usually end up with these because we were not able to get good Iron Condor trades as we tried to leg into them.

Delta Verticals we are trading at 66.67% success. Also, not a huge volume of trades.

Probability based Iron Condors, Broken Wing Iron Condors and Strangles we are at 90.00% as of this writing.

Calendar trades are at 58.70%, which is not very good.

Butterfly trades are at 85.71% but there are not a lot of these so we still need to wait and see as we are trading them more often now.

I hope you have enjoyed and more importantly learned something reviewing my trades. To me, the only thing better than reviewing a persons trade journal is watching them trade during real market conditions. I do post more current trades on my website. Not usually in as much detail as in this book but after reading this you can probably determine my thinking on my ongoing trades.

I encourage you to check out my website, www.trade4profits.com, for lots more trading information and ongoing trades. Learning to trade profitably is not always easy, but it is easier if you have a community supporting you.

If you have not read **Trade4Profits – Shortcuts to Profitable Trading** I urge you to do so. Shortcuts to Profitable trading will give you insights to many of the trades you have seen in this book. It will help you understand my basic trading philosophy and why I trade the way I do.

If you have not read **Trade4Profits – Watch Me Trade**, the one before this one. Then you should pick it up also. You will get to see some of the types of trades here. However, we were trading a little differently back then so you might learn something that is not in this book. You can decide which trading style you like best.

I urge you to follow my twitter account at trade4profits1 to see what I am currently trading.

You can find a link to my books at www.trade4profits.com or www.jddawson.net

Good luck with your trading and don't forget to keep your own trading journal!

Made in the USA
Las Vegas, NV
18 February 2022

44165029R00072